INTRODUCTION

To

LAW STUDY AND LAW EXAMINATIONS IN A NUTSHELL

With Illustrative Problems
And Answers

By

STANLEY V. KINYON
Professor of Law University of Minnesota

ST. PAUL, MINN.
WEST PUBLISHING CO.
1971

KInyon Intro.Law Study Nutshell
6th Reprint—1980

PREFACE

Back in 1939, not long after my own graduation from law school and as a young law teacher working with first-year law students, I sensed their need for a clear, non-technical explanation of the basic objectives and mechanics of professional law study and problem-type law exam questions. I envisioned a fairly comprehensive book, like this one, with extensive explanation of exam writing and numerous illustrations of typical exam problems and answers, to help the students adjust more quickly to what was expected of them in a professional law school. The need for such a book was not then clearly apparent and I could not persuade a publisher to undertake its publication.

The West Publishing Company, however, was willing to experiment on a limited scale, so I prepared for them my little booklet on HOW TO STUDY LAW AND WRITE LAW EXAMINATIONS as a sort of trial balloon. It was first published in 1940 and, with a minor revision in 1951, has been distributed to more than a half-million law students in the ensuing 31 years.

V

PREFACE

Despite its increasing inappropriateness for today's older and more sophisticated law school freshmen the demand for it has continued until the plates from which it has been printed have completely worn out and been discarded. Obviously the need for the larger, more comprehensive and up to date book has been demonstrated.

Two years ago, Mr. Noreen, head of the Law School Department at West (and a former student of mine, by the way), asked me to write such a book for their Nutshell Series, not realizing that this was the type of book I had originally hoped to write. Needless to say it has been a gratifying experience to bring to fruition an idea born so long ago.

I would be remiss in not acknowledging some valuable contributions to this volume. I am deeply indebted and truly grateful to the half-dozen able and experienced law professors from several different university law faculties who, for obvious reasons, shall remain unidentified but who generously took time to furnish me with typical problems they had recently prepared and used in their exams in traditional first-year subjects, with anonymous samples of what they regarded as good or marginal answers. From these, and some of my own, I selected, and edited in minor respects, the illustrative problems and answers in Part II of the book. These present, I believe, an interesting and representative sampling of the types of problems currently presented to first-year examinees by seasoned teachers. They depict a fairly broad panorama of styles of answer-writing and illustrate the range, from excellent to marginally acceptable, in substantive content and exposition. They should be helpful to beginners who really want some guidance in answering law exam problems.

June 3, 1971.   Stanley V. Kinyon

•

OUTLINE

		Page
Preface		V
INTRODUCTION		1
PART I. LAW STUDY IN LAW SCHOOLS		5
§ 1.	WHAT LAW STUDY IS ALL ABOUT	5
a.	"Law" and Legal Systems	5
b.	Types of Legal Rules	8
c.	Objectives of "The Law"	9
d.	Areas of Law	11
e.	Law Schools and The Legal Profession	17
f.	Object of Law Study	20
§ 2.	TOOLS AND SKILLS	22
a.	The Importance of Language to Lawyers and Law Students	22
b.	Reading Skills	24
c.	Writing Skills	27
d.	Using Law Books—"Finding The Law"	30

Page

§ 3. "CASES", "CASEBOOKS" AND THE "CASE METHOD" OF LAW STUDY _____ 31

a. The "Cases" in "Casebooks" ____ 34

b. Reading Cases _____ 40

c. "Briefing" Cases _____ 51

Illustrative Case _____ 54

Sample Brief _____ 58

d. "Canned Briefs" _____ 60

§ 4. CLASS WORK—TAKING NOTES —CLASS ATTENDANCE ____ 62

a. Teaching Methods _____ 62

b. Taking Notes _____ 63

c. Class Attendance and Importance 66

§ 5. SUPPLEMENTARY READING__ 70

§ 6. USING STUDENT TEXTBOOKS AND "HORNBOOKS" _____ 73

§ 7. REVIEW _____ 78

a. Day-to-Day Review _____ 79

b. Periodic Review _____ 82

c. Reviewing With Other Students— Discussions and Arguments ___ 87

§ 8. OUTLINES _____ 89

Illustrative Outline _____ 91

§ 9. STUDYING FOR EXAMS _____ 95

OUTLINE

Page

PART II. LAW EXAM PROBLEMS, ANSWERS AND COMMENTS ------------------ 101

INTRODUCTION TO PART II. --------- 101

§ 1. EXAMINATION OBJECTIVES AND LAW EXAM PROBLEM —QUESTIONS ---------------- 102

  a. Objectives of Examinations in General—Types of Questions -- 102

  b. Law Exams -------------------- 104

  c. What the Examiner Looks for in Answers to Problem Questions 108

  d. Writing the Answers ----------- 118
    1. Reading the Problem -------- 120
    2. Analysis ------------------- 121
      Illustrative Problem -------- 122
    3. Planning the Answer -------- 126
    4. Writing -------------------- 127

§ 2. ILLUSTRATIVE PROBLEM QUESTIONS WITH SAMPLE ANSWERS AND COMMENTS 129

CONTRACTS REMEDIES PROBLEM ------ 131
  Professor's Summary of Relevant Issues and Sub-Issues -------------- 134
  Good "A" Answer ------------------- 138
  Marginal Answer ------------------- 144

XI

OUTLINE

§ 2. ILLUSTRATIVE PROBLEM QUES-
TIONS WITH SAMPLE AN-
SWERS AND COMMENTS—Con-
tinued   **Page**

CONTRACTS (I) PROBLEM _____ 148
  Good "A" Answer _____ 150
  Marginal Answer _____ 156

CONTRACTS (II) PROBLEM _____ 159
  Good "A" Answer _____ 161
  Marginal Answer _____ 168

AGENCY (IN CONTRACT CASES) PROB-
LEM _____ 172
  Good "A" Answer _____ 174
  Marginal Answer _____ 178

TORTS—GENERAL COMMENT _____ 184

TORTS (I) PROBLEM _____ 185
  Good "A" Answer _____ 192
  Marginal Answer _____ 198

TORTS (II) PROBLEM _____ 207
  Good "A" Answer _____ 211
  Marginal Answer _____ 223

TORTS (III) PROBLEM _____ 228
  Good "A" Answer _____ 231
  Marginal Answer _____ 244

PROPERTY (I) PROBLEM _____ 251
  Professor's Analysis for Grading ____ 253
  Good "A" Answer _____ 258
  Marginal Answer _____ 262

OUTLINE

§ 2. ILLUSTRATIVE PROBLEM QUESTIONS WITH SAMPLE ANSWERS AND COMMENTS—Continued

Page

PROPERTY (II) PROBLEM _____ 266
  Good "A" Answer _____ 271
  Marginal Answer _____ 278

PROPERTY (III) PROBLEM _____ 286
  Good "A" Answer _____ 292
  Marginal Answer _____ 299

PROCEDURE (I) PROBLEM _____ 304
  Good "A" Answer _____ 305
  Marginal Answer _____ 307

PROCEDURE (II) PROBLEM _____ 309
  Good "A" Answer _____ 310
  Marginal Answer _____ 314

CONSTITUTIONAL LAW (I) PROBLEM ___ 316
  Good "A" Answer _____ 318
  Marginal Answer _____ 323

CONSTITUTIONAL LAW (II) PROBLEM __ 328
  Part A—Good "A" Answer _____ 332
        Marginal Answer _____ 339
  Part B—Good "A" Answer _____ 342
        Marginal Answer _____ 347

CRIMINAL LAW GENERAL COMMENT ____ 350

CRIMINAL LAW PROBLEM _____ 352
  Good "A" Answer _____ 361
  Marginal Answer _____ 365

INDEX _____ 369

INTRODUCTION TO
LAW STUDY
AND EXAMINATIONS

INTRODUCTION

This book, intended for first-year law students, is based upon the author's own experience, first as a law student and then as a teacher of first-year law students. It contains practical information, explanations and suggestions that have proved to be helpful to an early understanding of what law study and problem-type law exams are all about. No attempt is made to analyze or discuss the whole three-year program of professional law study or all of the things one will be expected to study and learn before graduation.

Part I on Law Study in Law Schools should be read at the beginning of the first year and carefully studied during the first confusing weeks in law school.

Part II on Law Exam Problems and Answers explains and illustrates the problem-type questions typically encountered both in first-year exams and also in bar examinations and contains sample answers for study in preparing for those exams.

You might ask why a book like this is needed. Law students today are typically adult college graduates with substantially better-than-average academic records and fairly high scores on legal aptitude tests. Most are mature, well-informed adults, many with substantial employment experience or military service, or both, and some already married and parents. Most have also become quite expert in the techniques of reading and comprehending educational text books, organizing, learning and remembering facts and information, and preparing for and answering successfully the typical, objective or essay examinations so common in undergraduate schooling. Such students need no explanation of those things.

Law study, however, is quite different in many respects from most undergraduate study. Even with conscientious effort and necessary legal aptitudes and college records, a significant number of students still flunk out of law school and too many achieve only mediocre records in their law study. Also, too high a percentage of those who do graduate fail the bar exam, at least on the first try. This suggests that many who have the aptitudes to be good lawyers plus motivation and good records of college achievement either fail to perceive fully or to adjust soon enough to the different methods and objectives of law study and examinations, and need more initial guidance in these matters than they usually get.

Law school will seem strange at first to most beginning students. Legal terminology is usually unfamiliar and so are the "cases" assigned for study. Classroom procedure is different and the expected amount and intensity of effort is high. Each course very quickly gets into meaty, complex, legal problems since there is no easy, logical or simple beginning point in studying law and the legal system.

The beginner usually hears dire predictions of failure and all sorts of rumors about the various professors, their idiosyncracies, and what he must do to "get by" with "Old So-andso". He is advised knowingly by advanced students about "canned briefs", outlines and various student texts that supposedly simplify and clarify everything. Despite

their use he usually finds that the results on
his first law exam are discouraging unless
he has received early and sound guidance as
to the objectives of law study, what he must
learn, how to study most effectively, what
the professors and, later, the bar examiners
are looking for in the examinations, and what
ultimately will be expected of him as a lawyer. Only with such guidance will he be able
to adjust quickly to law study and make the
best use of his talents. Hopefully the explanations, information and suggestions on
the following pages will provide the necessary
assistance.

PART I

LAW STUDY IN LAW SCHOOLS

SECTION 1. WHAT LAW STUDY IS ALL ABOUT

a. "Law" and Legal Systems

In beginning the study of law it is helpful to have a fairly clear understanding of what is meant by the term "law" as the subject of your study.

In its broadest sense "law" signifies any principle or rule governing or controlling something or someone. Thus, we speak of the "laws of nature", "law of gravity", "Mendel's law", "law of the jungle", "law of averages", etc., etc.

The law practiced by lawyers and dealt with in law schools, however, consists of *governmentally prescribed* rules and procedures governing *human activities* and *relations* in organized society, particularly the harmful and disruptive activities and those involving conflicts between people and controversies over the rightfulness or wrongfulness of various types of behavior.

[5]

There is an enormous body of these rules and procedures. They have been developed and promulgated over the years by various governmental bodies for a variety of reasons. Many embody customary practices based upon traditional beliefs and principles of fair play and justice. Others represent prevailing community mores, desires or needs. Some are based upon social and political policies, while many merely represent practical choices among acceptable alternatives where *some* rule is necessary. Broad basic rules have been adopted in our constitutions, State and Federal. Many rules and procedures of all types have been formally enacted in statutes by legislative bodies such as the United States Congress and the state legislatures or assemblies. Others have been enacted as ordinances by municipal councils or as regulations by administrative boards and commissions. In addition to these formal *statutory* rules created by legislation we have many rules and procedures in areas not governed by statutes that have been developed and followed by our courts and other legal tribunals in the process of deciding controversies brought to them for decision. These are found in the opinions written in support of their decisions and are usually referred to as

[6]

"common law" rules. They can be, and frequently are, changed or replaced by legislation. All of our rules and procedures are constantly being modified and changed as society grows and develops.

A complicating factor, of course, is that in the United States we have a complex, interrelated network of many governments—Federal, state and local—each with its own legislative, administrative and judicial bodies that make rules of law applicable in the area governed by each. Most state and local rules and procedures are not uniform throughout the country. Thus, "The Law" differs in many respects from state to state and locality to locality and this makes law study more difficult.

A further complication arises from the fact that lawyers and law schools are not and cannot be concerned solely with this mass of legal rules since the meaning and significance of the rules cannot be adequately understood apart from their *application*. This requires some understanding of the structure, powers, personnel and procedures of the various legislative and administrative bodies, courts and other legal tribunals, law enforcement agencies, penal and corrective institutions and other governmental organizations that make, interpret, apply and enforce the rules and operate in accordance with them.

Law study thus involves acquiring an understanding of our *whole legal process*—the legal systems, tribunals and institutions of our various governments, how they operate and the *procedural rules* governing their organization and operations as well as the *rules they apply* in determining the substantive rights, duties, powers and freedoms of the people they deal with, and the remedies available for, or *penalties* applicable to, violations of substantive rules.

b.   Types of Legal Rules

The total body of legal rules is thus comprised partly of *"substantive law"* (governing basic rights, powers, obligations, freedoms etc.), partly of *"procedural law"* (governing jurisdiction, operations and procedures of courts and other legal bodies) and partly of *"remedial law"* (governing remedies, penalties and other sanctions or consequences of law violation). These main categories, of course, overlap to some extent so that it is not always clear whether a particular rule is substantive, procedural or remedial. Many of your law school courses deal primarily with substantive rules, some deal primarily with procedure and a few primarily with remedies, but in each course you will encounter to some extent all three types.

c. Objectives of "The Law"

"The Law" in the broad sense of our whole legal system with its institutions, rules, procedures, remedies, etc., is society's attempt, through government, to control human behavior and prevent anarchy, violence, oppression and injustice by providing and enforcing orderly, rational, fair and workable alternatives to the indiscriminate use of force by individuals or groups in advancing or protecting their interests and resolving their controversies. "Law" seeks to achieve both social order and individual protection, freedom and justice.

In any society or group of people attempting to live and work together there will always be conflicts of interest, disputes and controversies over the inevitable interferences with each others' interests in freedom, person, property or wealth that occur even between honest, responsible people of good will. Most of these conflicts and disputes can

be, and are, resolved and settled by the people
involved, either by concession, compromise
or submission, without resort to legal procedures. When that is not possible or acceptable the disputants must, and will, resort
to the use of some type of force unless society
provides a satisfactory legal alternative, compels its use and punishes those who use force
to achieve their objectives and resolve their
disputes. Furthermore, in any group or society of any size there are always some anti-
social people who, either individually or in
groups, sometimes act so aggressively or
cruelly or dishonestly toward others or otherwise in such disregard for their safety, security or welfare as to cause death, injury,
property damage, economic loss, unreasonable fear or some other interference with social order and individual welfare. If such
anti-social, "criminal" behavior is not dis-
couraged, prevented, corrected, punished or
otherwise curtailed as far as possible through
public disapproval, corrective programs or
the use of the organized and ordered force of
society (police, possé, militia, army, etc.) it
will lead to terrorism, retaliation, injustice,
violence and anarchy.

"Law", therefore, does not involve an abandonment of physical force in resolving disputes or ·in curtailing anti-social behavior. Rather, it is an attempt, through government, to organize and control the physical force of society and use it when necessary to protect society and compel as far as possible adherence to rational and generally acceptable rules of behavior and orderly dispute-settling and enforcement procedures.

d. Areas of Law

There are two main and sometimes overlapping areas in which "The Law" seeks to achieve its sometimes conflicting objectives of social order and individual safety, freedom and justice: (1) the *"Criminal and Public Law"* area, and (2) the *"Private or Civil Law"* area. The first involves the direct relations and controversies between governments and private individuals or groups (Nation or State vs. Individual or Association or Private Corporation, and sometimes Government vs. Government). The second involves private relations and controversies between individuals or groups (Individual(s) vs. Individual(s), or Individual(s) vs. Private Corporation(s) or Association(s), or Private

Corporation(s) vs. Private Corporation(s), etc.) The latter may or may not initially involve any Public or Criminal Law or substantial interference with social order, but if not resolved peaceably, may in any case lead to violence, oppression and injustice.

Each of these main areas of "Law" has its own bodies of rules governing substance, procedure and remedies-or-penalties, and each is, in law books and law study, extensively divided and subdivided into numerous sub-areas and categories such as Criminal Law and Procedure, Administrative Law, Constitutional Law, Taxation, Utilities Regulation, etc. in the Criminal and Public Law area, and Contracts, Torts, Property, Civil Procedure, Remedies, Wills, Estates and Trusts, and others in the Private or Civil Law area.

Criminal and Public Law involves statutory or administrative prohibitions, regulations or requirements imposed directly by governments or government agencies upon individuals, or associations or corporations, or other governmental bodies. Violations of some of these are deemed public offenses and classified as "crimes", major or minor, with specified penalties imposed through public prosecutions and convictions in criminal

trials. Violations of many types of regulations prescribed by government agencies are
not public offenses or crimes subject to prosecution. These are dealt with by administrative orders or other sanctions or enforcement procedures.

Private or Civil Law involves a multitude of
rules applicable to the innumerable activities,
encounters and transactions between people
in their various societal relations on the basis
of which disputes between them can be avoided, settled, or resolved by agreement or by
private law-suits, on a fair and rational basis
consistent with accepted principles of justice
and social policy or expedience.

The distinctions between the areas of Public and Criminal Law and Private or Civil
Law, of course, are necessarily somewhat
arbitrary and artificial. A given type of activity or behavior may violate a criminal
statute, or an administrative regulation, or
both, and also constitute a private wrong to
an individual harmed by it. Also, a government often acts in a purely private capacity
in making a contract with, or buying property from, an individual or private organization and sometimes becomes involved in what
is essentially a Private or Civil Law dispute

over the transaction. Nevertheless, the distinctions serve a useful purpose since the objectives, procedures and sanctions in criminal prosecutions, administrative hearings and private law suits are quite different in many respects.

Perhaps the interrelationship between substantive, procedural and remedial law, discussed earlier, and these major areas of Criminal and Public and Private or Civil Law can be helpfully illustrated by the accompanying diagram in which the whole enclosure represents all of "The Law" and is divided into substantive, procedural and remedial law on one axis and the areas of Public and Criminal and Private or Civil Law on the other:

	Substantive Law	Procedural Law	Remedial Law
Private or Civil Law (Individual or Group or Organization vs. Individual or Group or Organization)	Contracts Torts Property Agency-Employment Corporations Trusts & Estates Commercial Law other private law subjects	Jurisdiction Pleading Evidence Trial Procedure Appellate Procedure Judgments Decrees, Writs, etc. Motions, Petitions Replevin, Unlawful Detainer, etc.	Damages Injunction Specific performance Restitution Eviction, etc.
Criminal and Public Law (Government vs. Individual or Group or Organization or other Government)	Criminal Law Constitutional Law Administrative Law Taxation Welfare Law Anti-Trust Law other public law subjects	Criminal Jurisdiction & Procedure: Arrest Indictment Arraignment Criminal Trial Procedure Evidence Criminal Appeals Habeas Corpus, etc. Administrative Hearings, Appeals & other proceedings	Criminal Penalties: Fine Imprisonment Probation Parole, etc. Administrative Cease-and-desist Orders, etc. Mandamus & other Extraordinary Remedies

This sort of illustration, of course, is incomplete and cannot show all of the subjects, subdivisions, overlapping and interrelations between categories. It merely gives a rough, general idea of the major types, areas and subjects of law. Some courses in law school deal primarily with Private or Civil Law; others primarily with Criminal or Public Law; some deal primarily with substantive rules; others mainly with procedural, and so on, but there is much overlap.

In studying law one must remember that governments and "The Law", like other institutions created and operated by fallible human beings, are neither perfect nor immutable and embody many human imperfections, inconsistencies, errors and prejudices. Thus, they often fail to achieve adequately their objectives of maintaining order, resolving controversies promptly and fairly, and doing justice through appropriate restraints and redress of grievances. When these failures occur there is a breakdown of "law and order" and many otherwise law-abiding people may resort to self-help or to force and violence to resolve their conflicts and resist oppression and injustice. To remedy these defects and develop a more just and effective legal process for reconciling the conflicting interests, desires, policies and beliefs of an ever more populous and complex society is the continuing challenge to the legal profession and to others engaged in the governmental activities that make, change and administer "The Law".

e. Law Schools and the Legal Profession

No person can learn all about "The Law" in a lifetime, much less in three or four years in a law school. Furthermore, "studying law" in a law school involves much more than merely acquiring some understanding of our legal systems and learning some of the basic rules in the major divisions and areas of law as a part of one's general education.

Law schools are high-standard *professional schools*. Many of them today operate at the graduate level and require for admission a baccalaureate degree with high levels of academic achievement plus superior professional aptitudes. They are established for, and devote their efforts primarily to, the basic "groundschool" professional education and training of lawyers, just as medical schools are primarily involved in the basic professional education and training of medical doctors. Such training involves not only the thorough learning of a considerable amount of technical, professional information and terminology but also, and more importantly, it requires learning the basic professional skills and techniques necessary to *apply* this knowledge in performing professional tasks as paid experts.

Lawyers are the experts largely responsible for the effective operation of our legal systems. As judges they preside over the courts and are expected to apply the rules of law properly in resolving the public and private controversies brought before them for decision. Many legislators, government officials and administrators are lawyers, and many government agencies employ legal counsel to advise them on the proper performance of their functions and represent them in controversies. Most lawyers, of course, participate in the legal system by "practicing law" either in private law firms or in the legal departments of corporations or government agencies. Law practice consists of furnishing, for compensation, legal advice, services and representation to those who need it: advising and counseling people, organizations or governmental departments or agencies on their legal rights, freedoms and obligations; preparing legal documents and instruments of all kinds for them; negotiating for them in many transactions and controversies and representing them as advocates in disputes before courts and other tribunals to insure that their rights, freedoms and obligations are protected and enforced in accordance with law.

Lawyers are primarily expert *legal problem-solvers* and *advocates* for those who retain or employ them as such. In addition, upon admission to practice, they also become officers of the courts and members of a governmentally-licensed profession with prescribed standards of competence, ethical behavior and responsibility for the advancement of justice. Through bar associations and other professional and civic organizations lawyers are continually engaged in various types of law-reform and law-improvement activities. People expect from lawyers the best effort and expertise of which each is capable, both in public service and in protecting the lives, safety, freedoms and economic interests entrusted to them by clients. No one will willingly pay a lawyer for mediocre or incompetent work or for less than his best and most skillful effort. Law study thus requires the best effort you can give it, not just enough to "get by" and "pass the course". Professional standards are high.

f. Object of Law Study

From what has been said about law, lawyers and law schools, it should be obvious to you that studying law in law school involves much more than merely memorizing a flock of legal terms and rules and acquiring information about our legal systems. It involves some of that but also involves the much more exacting task of learning how the legal process works and how to participate in it as a lawyer; how to analyze a legal problem; where and how to *find* the rules and decisions applicable to that particular type of problem; how to *reason* from these to *conclusions* and possible *solutions* of the problem; and how to *apply* the analysis, reasoning and conclusions in advising a client, or in writing an opinion, or in drafting required instruments, or in negotiating a transaction or representing a client in a lawsuit, hearing, prosecution or appeal or other legal proceeding, or in doing the other things that lawyers are employed and expected to do.

Since lawyers always deal with specific legal problems brought to them for solution, law study and teaching is largely problem-and-case oriented. Study and class discussion are focused primarily on series of related fact

[*20*]

situations involving controversies and disputes over the legality of what has happened or is proposed or desired in each situation. Some of the situations are hypothetical but many have been involved in actual court cases or other legal proceedings and the study and discussion involves critical analyses of such decisions and opinions and the rules and reasoning relied on by the courts in reaching their conclusions. We will shortly consider in some detail what is involved in proper case-reading and analysis.

From such study and analysis, students with sufficient analytic, diagnostic and reasoning aptitudes for a professional level of performance, can learn how to reason out and predict the probable solutions of legal problems in various situations and develop the other professional skills they will need to begin the practice of law.

Try always to remember that as a law student you are not concerned so much with *what* "The Law" *is* as you are with *how it works* and how *you* will *work with it as a lawyer*.

Remember, also, that "The Law" you are studying is not immutable or static. It is and must be a dynamic, constantly growing and

developing human institution. As such it
has many human imperfections, faults and
shortcomings and can grow worse rather than
better unless the legal profession, the legislators and others who control, operate and
guide it constantly strive to improve it and
make it a better instrument of justice. As
a law student, therefore, you must not only
be concerned with how it *now* operates but
also with its present imperfections and how
it can be changed and improved to better
achieve both social order and the individual
protections and freedoms we desire. Lawyers
should not be simply advocates and defenders
of the *status quo*. They must, of course, understand and work with "The Law" as it is,
but they should be constantly alert to its
needed improvements and strive to achieve
them by legal means.

SECTION 2. TOOLS AND SKILLS

a. The Importance of Language to Lawyers and Law Students

Analytically, the ingredients of "The Law"
—the basic stuff out of which its rules and
procedures are fabricated—consist of a vast
complex of ideas, concepts, beliefs and conclusions as to what is proper and improper

behavior in the innumerable activities and
relationships in a governmentally organized
society. These products of the thinking of
law-makers, judges and lawyers over the cen-
turies have been formulated, expressed and
communicated in *words*, in written and spoken *language*, much of which has been printed and preserved in the millions of documents, reports and legal publications, official
and unofficial, that constitute our legal literature.

It is these ideas, concepts and beliefs, embodied in propositions, arguments and rule-
conclusions, expressed in the language of legal documents and law-books, that lawyers
and judges study, analyze and apply in their
professional work and that law students study
and work with in law school. The subject
matter and raw material of "The Law" is
thus embodied and expressed in *the language
of the lawbooks*—the statute books, reports
of decisions and opinions of courts and other
tribunals, legislative records, legal encyclopedias, digests, treatises, textbooks, casebooks, law reviews, etc. The law library is
the lawyer's and law student's warehouse,
workshop and laboratory. It is there they
find the materials on which their work is
based; there they do the studying, analyzing

and thinking, and there they draft the writings that embody the products of their study and thought.

b. Reading Skills

The first basic skill, therefore, that you need to develop as a law student is skill in the type of intensive, critical, painstaking reading of legal publications, instruments and documents that lawyers must do. It is vastly more exacting than most of the reading you've previously done.

First, of course, you have a problem of *vocabulary*—learning the precise meaning of the numerous technical terms used by lawyers. Many of these legal terms will be wholly new and strange to you—some propositions, inherited from the past, are even expressed in Latin. Other terms are familiar words used in common speech which have acquired a different and special meaning in law. With either you will need a good legal dictionary—like the one-volume Black's Law Dictionary—and will need to use it constantly during your first months in law school and thereafter whenever you encounter unfamiliar terms. Although law schools generally do not require that each student purchase a legal dictionary, since copies are normally

[24]

provided in the school library, buying one of your own is a worthwhile investment if you can afford it. You'll need it continually both as law student and lawyer. Precision in understanding and using terms is the earmark of a good lawyer.

Your next task is learning to read law books and other legal writings *intensively*, *analytically* and *critically*. Law books purport to convey either rules or regulations, or carefully stated facts, or closely reasoned analyses, arguments and propositions relating to various types of fact situations, behavior, rules, procedures, etc. In reading statutes or other formally prescribed rules, legal descriptions, deeds, wills, contracts, examination problems and the like, *every word* is important and must be considered carefully as to its scope and precise meaning. In reading opinions, briefs, textbooks and articles in legal periodicals it is essential that you clearly *understand* the writer's propositions, follow each step in his reasoning and analysis, grasp the distinctions and qualifications he sometimes expresses in a single word or phrase, and comprehend his conclusions and assertions. It is also essential to do this critically and questioningly, and not simply accept passively what is said.

You must learn to *think actively* when you are reading legal writings. Question all asserted propositions; look for faulty logic or unjustified assumptions in arguments; test conclusions against the background of your own experience and beliefs and what you have learned from other sources, and try to formulate opposing arguments and conclusions. The things expressed in legal opinions, text books and articles are simply the ideas and beliefs, arguments, observations and conclusions of the writer—a non-omniscient, fallible human being—who may be wrong and cannot possibly comprehend any fact or problem from *all* points of view or on the basis of all human experience.

There is seldom one *best* rule or solution for any legal problem. The task of the legal profession is to explore, ascertain and examine all of the *possibly adequate* or *appropriate* solutions and try to expound and establish the one that seems most appropriate for each situation and problem. The good lawyer is one who always challenges assumptions, premises, arguments and conclusions—his own as well as those of others—seeking and considering all plausible possibilities and accepting none until it stands up under comparison and critical analysis.

c. Writing Skills

Skillful reading of law books and other legal writings of course is only part of the language skills needed by lawyers. Legal language is not merely the source and subject matter of law and law study; it is also the basic *tool* of the legal profession. Lawyers do not use scalpels, slide-rules, test tubes or other mechanical apparatus in their work. Their tools are *words*, carefully chosen and put together to communicate and implement their analyses of problems. Written and spoken words, in various forms, are the media in which they give legal advice and opinions, present arguments, draft documents, instruments and agreements, try lawsuits, write briefs and perform other professional tasks. Words are also the conduit for law school study and learning; the means by which lectures and recitations are given, class discussion carried on, notes taken, outlines prepared, examinations written, etc.

In a very real sense lawyers are language-craftsmen and word-merchants, not in the manner of poets, novelists, historians or newsmen, but in articulating problems, expressing rules, presenting arguments, stating reasons and drafting the various documents and written instruments employed in legal proceedings and needed by the individuals, groups, businesses and governments they represent and serve.

Many people think of lawyers as being primarily skilled orators addressing courts and juries. This, of course, they do at times, but the overwhelming bulk of their work is embodied in various types of legal writing and drafting. They must thus possess not only highly developed reading, analytical and reasoning skills but consummate skill in clear, persuasive, expository writing. They must develop great expertise in the meaning and selection of words and in their grammatical organization—not to present word-pictures but to express ideas and reasons, intentions and propositions, so clearly and unambiguously that misunderstanding is minimized and maximum communication is achieved. It should be clear from this that law study involves intensive practice in expository legal writing.

In law school, therefore, after you have mastered the basic legal vocabulary and developed some technique in reading and analyzing court opinions, statutes and other legal writings, you must start developing your own abilities to express legal ideas, reasoning and conclusions in writing. You will need some skill in this type of writing to prepare clear and accurate condensed statements ("briefs") of the court opinions in your casebooks (explained in the next section) for class discussion and review. You will need more of such skill to write proper answers to the problem questions on your law school exams (discussed in Part II of this book), to prepare appropriate papers in courses in legal research and writing and to draft the agreements, documents, appeal briefs and other legal instruments you will be assigned to prepare in advanced courses, seminars, "legal aid", "law review" and other practical legal work.

Too many beginning law students have never developed much skill in expository writing—expressing ideas, reasoning, arguments and conclusions in clear, accurate, well-organized statements couched in appropriate language grammatically correct. A high degree of such skill is essential for competent lawyers and *can be developed* by people with adequate aptitude for law study. So, if you are one of those who have difficulty "saying what you mean" in writing you will need to devote considerable time and thought and practice to the improvement of your writing ability. As a lawyer you must be a skilled craftsman in this respect.

d.   Using Law Books—"Finding The Law"

Most of the basic, first-year law school courses—Contracts, Torts, Property, etc.— are taught from "casebooks" or "course-books" which you will be required to buy. A number of the later courses are also taught from such books. They are discussed in some detail in the next section of this book. Most of your first year reading assignments will be in them, but you will also be assigned to read some sections in the state or federal statute books, and references will be made occasionally to treatises, textbooks, law-review articles and other law books containing relevant material. These you will find in the school library and will not be expected to purchase. In many subjects there are good, one-volume student texts or "Hornbooks", prepared by legal scholars and presenting somewhat summary discussions of the more important areas of the subjects. The use of these in your study is discussed in Section 6, below.

Since law books are the sources of "The Law", and since the law library is the laboratory of the lawyer and law student, another of your important tasks in law school is to learn about the various types of law books and develop skill in using them. Knowing how to "Find the Law" on any particular problem—the relevant statutes, "cases" and text discussions—is an essential legal skill, and most schools have courses dealing with legal bibliography and research to help you develop it. These tend to be very time-consuming and not particularly inspiring. They require a lot of what seems like tedious effort in looking for and examining dusty books in the library, and trying to figure out how each is organized and indexed, how to find specific materials in them, how to cite them, etc. But don't neglect this learning or give it only superficial attention and effort. Most of the specific problems you'll encounter as a lawyer will involve law you have not studied in school, and to solve those problems you will have to *find the applicable law.* Being able to do that quickly, thoroughly and efficiently is probably the most useful mechanical skill you can acquire apart from skill in legal reading and writing.

SECTION 3. "CASES", "CASEBOOKS" AND THE "CASE METHOD" OF LAW STUDY

Most law schools in this country, in their basic first-year courses and in some subsequent courses, use what is known as the "case method" of instruction. Under this method most of the study materials for each course are organized and presented in a "casebook" that has been prepared by a legal scholar or scholars specializing in the subject matter of the course. The material in these "casebooks" consists mainly of verbatim reproductions of the published reports of decisions and opinions written by judges in deciding "cases" —i. e. legal controversies—that have been brought to the courts. Lawyers use the term "case" to refer both to a whole legal controversy and also to the written reported opinion and decision when the controversy has been taken to court. In view of this dual meaning of the term it would be more accurate to speak of "opinion books" and studying court "opinions", but "case" and "casebook" are the terms used and we will consider in some detail what these "cases" are, what's in them and how to read and analyze them in beginning your study.

This "case method" of legal instruction is used for several reasons. It emphasizes the fact that professional legal work is essentially problem-oriented—always involving some problem or controversy ("case"), actual or potential, brought to the lawyer for solution.

Also, in requiring critical discussion and analysis of the actual decisions and reasoning of courts in specific, real-life controversies the "case method" provides perhaps the best basis not only for understanding what "The Law" *is* and *why,* but also for considering and discussing what it *should be* in such situations, thus developing skills and insights in law improvement. Furthermore, courts tend to follow their reasoning and decisions in prior cases when deciding later, similar cases. This is the principle of *stare decisis* (stand by decided cases; follow precedent). Consequently, when a lawyer gets a problem or controversy he looks for and studies, carefully, prior similar cases in the reported decisions to help him analyze his problem or case and try to predict how a court would probably decide it. Since accurate case reading and analysis is thus a technique that lawyers constantly employ, law schools have concluded that the best way for prospective lawyers to learn it is to use it in studying "The Law", at least in the basic law school courses, and at the same time learn how the courts actually decide cases of various types.

By studying and abstracting ("briefing") these opinions, studying the supplementary notes and text in the casebook, discussing these and the instructor's questions and comments about them in class, asking questions, taking notes and then comparing and putting them together through systematic reviewing and outlining, a student can learn the legal principles, policies, rules and reasons relied upon by courts in reaching decisions in various types of problems and get some understanding of how "The Law" works, the techniques of judges and lawyers, and how to go about reasoning out the solutions for new legal problems.

a. The "Cases" in "Casebooks"

The opinions—"cases"—in each casebook deal with various types of controversies that have arisen in the particular area(s) of law dealt with in the course (contracts, property, criminal law, procedure, etc.). The authors have selected them out of the thousands of cases in the printed reports either because they are "leading" cases in certain areas or typically representative of particular types of controversy, or because the opinion is concise or contains a particularly good (or bad) explanation of the law or example of legal reasoning, or because the facts are novel or interesting, or the decision is surprising, etc. He has found the cases through the various

legal "finding" books: digests, legal encyclopedias, treatises, annotations, etc. and has
arranged them under various headings and
in sequences designed to present a coherent
picture and sampling of the law in each division of the course.

Sometimes the author reproduces the
whole opinion as originally published; sometimes he omits some of the court's citations
to other cases, or portions of the opinion not
relevant to the particular topic in the casebook; sometimes he condenses in his own
words an unduly lengthy statement of the
facts or otherwise edits the opinion; but such
omissions or condensations are always indicated by asterisks, brackets or dots. Thus,
a principal case that you read in your casebook is normally an exact copy of all or part
of what some court has stated in deciding a
case. In some casebooks, to save space, the
author will reproduce one or more full opinions on a problem and then add his own short
abstracts of the opinions and decisions in other similar cases to give you a sampling of the
range of decisions on that particular type of
problem without having to read so many full
opinions.

The cases reproduced in your casebook are
usually taken from the printed reports of *ap-*

pellate opinions and decisions—i. e. decisions and opinions of higher courts in cases that have been *appealed* from lower or trial court decisions.

Trial court decisions (those rendered in the first court to which the controversy was taken) are not ordinarily recorded in printed volumes for public distribution, except in the Federal courts, New York, and a few other states. In most jurisdictions the pleadings, orders, verdicts, judgments, etc., in the trial courts are merely filed in bundles in the office of the clerk of the court, and the record of the proceedings at trial remains in stenotype tape or in shorthand in the court reporter's notebook unless a case is appealed. In that event, however, the appealing party has the record transcribed, printed and sent to the proper appellate court. Printed briefs are also usually submitted by each party to that court setting forth the arguments pro and con and the authorities relied on. Each party then has an opportunity for oral argument before the appellate court judges at a time prescribed by them. After the arguments have been heard, the judges meet in conference and come to some conclusion as to their decision. One of them is assigned the task of writing a statement of the decision and the court's reasons for making it. This is called the *opinion,* and when he has finished writing it he submits it to the other members of the court who either approve it, suggest changes, or dissent, in which case they may write a dissenting opinion of their own. After the majority of the judges have approved an opinion, it is "handed down" together with any dissenting opinions. That is, it is given out to the parties and made public in one way or another. Sometimes, as has been traditional in the United States Supreme Court, the opinions are read from the bench or summarized orally by the judge writing them; usually they are merely given to the clerk of the appellate court, who makes copies, sends one to each party concerned, and provides others for advance reporting through various agencies. The clerk keeps the opinions in each case decided by the court until a number have accumulated, and then has them edited and published in a volume— ordinarily in the order in which they were handed down. These volumes of "official reports", called the "state reports" where the decisions are those of state courts, are numbered consecutively. There is a series of reports published by the West Publishing Company, called the National Reporter System, which contains, in complete and accurate form, all state and federal decisions. Each unit of this system combines the opinions from a group of jurisdictions.[1] There are also several systems of selected reports which publish only those state or federal opinions

[1] Following is a list of the Reporters and the jurisdictions which they cover:

Atlantic		North Eastern	
Connecticut	New Hampshire	Illinois	Massachusetts
Delaware	New Jersey	Indiana	New York
Maine	Pennsylvania	Ohio	
Maryland	Rhode Island		
	Vermont		

District of Columbia
(*Municipal Court of Appeals*)

West's California Reporter	Southern	
California Supreme Court	Alabama	Louisiana
District Courts of Appeal	Florida	Mississippi
Superior Court, Appellate Department		

South Eastern		Pacific	
Georgia	South Carolina	Alaska	Montana
North Carolina	Virginia	Arizona	Nevada
	West Virginia	California	New Mexico
		(Sup.Ct. only)	Oklahoma
South Western		Colorado	Oregon
Arkansas	Missouri	Hawaii	Utah
Kentucky	Tennessee	Idaho	Washington
	Texas	Kansas	Wyoming

New York Supplement	Federal
Court of Appeals	U. S. Court of Appeals
Appellate Divisions	U. S. Court of Claims
Miscellaneous	U. S. Court of Customs & Patent Appeals

North Western	
Iowa	Nebraska
Michigan	North Dakota
Minnesota	South Dakota
	Wisconsin

Federal Supplement
U. S. District Courts
U. S. Customs Court

Federal Rules Decisions
U. S. District Courts
U. S. Supreme Court

considered to be of special significance. Thus,
an opinion handed down by most state courts
in this country will be published in at least
two sets of books, and sometimes in three or
more. After they are published, these opinions or "cases" are customarily referred to or
"cited" by giving the name of the case, the
volume number, name and page of the state
report in which it is published if it was decided by a state court, the volume number,
name and page of the particular unit and
series of the National Reporter System in
which it is reported, the volume number,
name and page of any other selected case
series in which it may have been published
and the date it was decided. For example:

MORTON v. WOOLERY, 48 N.D. 1132,

189 N.W. 232, 24 A.L.R. 1107 (1922)

The citation of a case decided in a *Federal*
District Court or Court of Appeals frequently will refer only to *one* set of reports—the

Federal Supplement or the Federal Reporter
—but will usually contain a reference, in connection with the date, to the particular federal court in which it was decided. For example:

ANDERSON v. LANE, 97 F.Supp. 265

name of case / volume number / Federal Supplement Reporter / page

(E.D.So.Car. 1951).

U. S. District Court for Eastern District of South Carolina / date decided

HUDSON v. LEWIS, 188 F.2d 679

name of case / volume / Federal Reporter 2nd Series / page

(5 Cir. 1951).

U. S. Court of Appeals for 5th Circuit / date

b. Reading Cases

Having briefly considered what these cases
are, how they came to be written and where
the authors of our casebooks found them, we
are ready to tackle the problem of how to

read them intelligently. No doubt you will be told that you must concentrate when you read, that you must read carefully and thoroughly, that you must try to understand what you read, that you must look up in the law dictionary the words you don't understand, and so forth and so on. Doing all those things is of course essential, but they alone won't make you an intelligent case reader or a good law student. The fundamental thing in reading cases is to know *what to look for*. Otherwise you may concentrate on the wrong thing or miss an important point.

Perhaps the best way to explain what to look for is to point out *what you can normally expect to find* in a case and what the judge normally puts or tries to put in his opinion.

1. The first thing you will usually find in a case is a brief statement of the kind of controversy involved. That is, whether it was a criminal prosecution, an action of tort for damages, an action for breach of contract, or to recover land, etc. This is usually accompanied by an explanation of how the case got to this particular court,[2] whether it started there, or, if it is a matter on appeal

---

[2] See "Jurisdiction in a Nutshell" by Ehrenzweig and Louisell, a succinct text for students.

(as it usually is), how and why it happened to get there, whether plaintiff or defendant appealed, and to just what action of the lower court the appealing party is objecting. For example: "This is an appeal by defendant from an adverse judgment," or "from an order of the lower court denying his motion for new trial," or "from an order of the lower court overruling his demurrer to the complaint," etc. These facts are frequently found in a preliminary paragraph prepared by the clerk of the court and inserted before the judge's opinion. Nevertheless, since they tell you just how that particular court came to consider the controversy and just what it had to decide, they are extremely important and should not be overlooked or passed over lightly.

The normal function of an appellate court is to review the proceedings of the lower court to determine whether prejudicial error was committed, not to re-try the case or re-determine the facts. If there was no prejudicial error, the lower court's decision stands and is affirmed since the parties "had their day in court" according to law and are not entitled to another trial. Only if there was *error* in the lower court's actions or rulings, so that one or both parties did not get a proper determination of the case in accordance with applicable law is the appellate court entitled to *reverse* the decision. If a new trial is necessary, the case is remanded to the trial court for this. The appealing party is normally required to specify the errors that he claims were committed, and these raise the immediate issues on appeal—i. e. whether the lower court committed error in the specified actions.

2. The next thing you will usually find is a statement of the *facts* of the controversy— who the parties were, what they did, what happened to them, who brought the action and what he wanted. Normally, the judge writing the opinion starts off with a complete statement of the facts, but judges are not always careful to do this and you will frequently find the facts strewn throughout the opinion. Sometimes significant facts are mentioned only in a dissenting opinion. Thus you can never be sure you know all about the controversy until you have read the whole opinion and any dissenting opinions. Sometimes the statement of facts is made categorically on the basis of the court's or jury's *findings* of fact; sometimes it is made by stating what the plaintiff and defendant *alleged* in their pleadings; and sometimes it is

in the form of a *resumé* of the *evidence* produced at trial. Wherever they may appear, however, and in whatever form they may be stated, every case contains some statement of the facts and circumstances out of which the controversy arose.

3. Next comes a statement of the question or questions the court is called upon to decide—the various "issues" (either of law or fact) which must be settled before a decision on the controversy can be reached. Any of you who have done any debating understand "issues"—the breaking up of a general problem into specific sub-problems. Some judges are very careful to state the issues clearly; others will leave them to inference from the discussion, or else wander around from one thing to another and leave the precise questions they are deciding in doubt. Sometimes the issues will be brought out by summarizing the *contentions* of each party.

4. After the issues comes the argument on each of them—a discussion of the pros and cons. This is where logic comes into play. You'll recall that there are two main types of logical reasoning—inductive and deductive. Inductive reasoning involves the

formulation of general propositions from a
consideration of specific problems or observations; deductive reasoning involves the *application* of a general proposition already
formulated to some specific situation or problem so that a conclusion can be drawn as to
it. In each case the court, having these definite and specific issues or problems to decide,
decides or purports to decide them by first
concluding what the general rule or proposition of law is as to this type of issue and the
reasons or policies underlying it (major
premise), and then deducing the decision on
that issue from the general rule on the basis
of the *facts* of the case (minor premise). If
there happens to be a statute or constitutional provision prescribing a general rule as to
questions like those involved in the case, the
judge has his major premise unless there is a
dispute over its meaning and an issue of interpretation on which cases involving its interpretation, if any, must be considered. Otherwise the judge will devote his argument to
a consideration of its scope and applicability
to the facts of the case. If there is no statute or other prescribed general rule, the judge
will try by induction to derive one from the
decisions and opinions in previous cases involving issues similar to those in the present

case, or from general principles of fairness, policy and common sense, and then apply it to the facts of the case and deduce his conclusion.

5. Finally, after the argument on all the issues (and sometimes a good deal of irrelevant argument and discussion), the judge states the *general* conclusion(s) to be drawn therefrom, and winds up the opinion with a statement of the court's decision. For example: "Judgment affirmed;" "Judgment reversed;" "Case remanded;" "New trial ordered;" etc.

It is to be remembered, of course, that legal opinions do not all follow the same order and are not all cut from the same pattern. They are written by many different judges, each of whom has his own style of writing and his own particular method of presenting a legal argument. Some opinions are not as easy to understand as others and it would be erroneous to assume in reading them that they are all correct and errorless. Courts frequently disagree as to the principles that ought to be applied in certain types of controversy and occasionally the same court will change its view as to the law on a particular point. In reading these cases, you are not trying to find *the* ultimate and perfect rule, you are trying to learn by *inductive* reasoning from what various courts have actually decided in particular cases the rules and principles most frequently applied and most likely to be applied by them in future cases of that type.

Now, having in mind what you can expect to find in the cases, and also the fact that they are not necessarily perfect and seldom embody an unchanging principle or universal truth, you are in a position to read them intelligently. It's not a bad idea, however, to adopt a systematic method of reading them. The following has proved effective, and you might try it as a starter.

First, get a clear picture of the controversy involved. Get all the facts and issues straight. Consider the following:

> What kind of an action or proceeding it was,
>
> Who the parties were,
>
> What they did and what happened to them,
>
> Who started the action or proceeding, what was sought, what the defense was,

What happened in the lower court (if it's a case on appeal),

How the case got to this court,

Just what this court had to decide in view of the claimed errors below.

At this point stop for a moment. Look at the problem, first from the plaintiff's or prosecution's point of view, then from the defendant's. Ask yourself how *you* would decide it, what *you* think the decision ought to be. Compare this case with others you have studied on the same topic. What result do *they* indicate ought to be reached here. Then, perhaps you may want to turn to the end of the opinion and see what *decision* the court reached. By doing these things you put yourself in a better position to read the court's argument critically, and spot any fallacies in it. We are all somewhat prone to accept what we read in print as the Gospel, and this little device of considering the problem and the court's decision in your own mind *before* reading the court's *argument* is a rather effective means of keeping a critical attitude.

Now read the court's argument, reasoning and conclusions. Consider the various rules and propositions advanced on each issue and analyze carefully the reasons given for adopting them, if the court gave reasons. See whether the conclusions drawn follow logically from those rules and reasons. Then ask yourself whether you agree with the court, and if not, why not. Consider also how the result in this case lines up with other similar cases you have studied.

In thus analysing the court's argument and conclusions it is important to distinguish carefully between the rules and propositions of law *actually relied upon by the court* in deciding the *issues involved in the case* (these are called *"holdings"*) and other legal propositions and discussion which you may find in the opinion but which are *not relevant nor applicable to the issues before the court* (these are called *"dicta"*). When the case was before the court, counsel for the opposing parties probably availed themselves of the opportunity to prepare fully and present to the court their arguments pro and con *upon the issues involved in it,* and the court thus had the opportunity to consider all aspects of each issue, choose the better result and "hold" with that view. *Dicta,* however, not being relevant to the issues before the court, was probably not argued by counsel nor thoroughly considered by the court. It was not *necessary* to the decision of the case and the court may have stated it casually without considering all aspects of the problem. Courts in each jurisdiction tend to regard their own prior "holdings" as creating *precedents* which they feel obliged to follow in later cases involving similar facts and the same issues unless circumstances or policies have materially changed since the earlier decision. This is the doctrine of *stare decisis* mentioned earlier and makes for stability and predictability in the law. *Dicta,* on the other hand, being casual and not a matter of *actual decision,* is *not* regarded as establishing law which will be binding on the court in a subsequent case. Thus, the former case containing the *dictum* is not a controlling "authority" on the question although it may be followed in later decisions.

You may find it very helpful, in picking out the important matters in the cases and in weeding out the irrelevant, to keep a pen or pencil handy and *underline* all statements of pertinent facts, issues, rules, etc. as you read. (Do this only *in your own casebooks,* however. *Do not mark or deface books in the library or elsewhere which are for common use!!!*)

Finally, study carefully any *notes, comment, text and abstracts* of other cases which the author may have appended to the case. They contain a good deal of valuable information and frequently suggest problems and criticisms which might not occur to you. There is an increasing tendency among the authors of casebooks to put in considerable supplementary matter along with the cases in order to clarify their significance. This matter is there for your benefit; take advantage of it!

If you adopt some such method as the above in reading your cases and acquire the habit of following it you are much more likely to get an accurate understanding of each case and are much less apt to overlook some important detail. Furthermore, if you get out of each case all the things mentioned above, you can feel reasonably well *prepared* for class discussion or lecture.

c. "Briefing" Cases

The term "briefing" a case, as used by law students, simply means making a brief written summary or abstract of the case in your own words—not the making of the printed "brief" (argument) which a lawyer submits to the court on behalf of his client. "Briefing" the cases in your casebook serves two purposes. First, and most important, it makes you read the case more thoroughly and carefully because you have to go back and dig out the essentials, organize them and state them in your own words. Second, it gives you a permanent condensed written record of each case which you can put in your notebook and use to refresh your memory about the case in the future without having to go back and read the whole opinion.

There are three cardinal rules to follow if you want to make good briefs:

1. *Don't try to brief the case as you read it through the first time!* Read it clear through (underlining if you wish) and then start your brief.

2. *Write the brief in your own words— don't just copy parts of the opinion.* A brief is an *abstract* or condensation of the case, not merely a bunch of quotations from it. Make sure, however, that your own statements are *accurate*.

3. *Organize your brief—Put in all essential matters in logical order, but be as concise as you can.* The ideal brief states all the essentials in logical order and without excess verbiage.

So far as this third rule is concerned a good logical order for a brief is as follows: *Type of Action—Facts—Issues—Decision—Reasons*.

As to the *Facts,* remember that they should include not only who the parties were and what happened to them, but also who brought suit, what sort of an action it was, what the defense was, and what happened to the controversy up to the time it reached this court. Thus, where the case is one on appeal, the statement of facts should include what happened in the lower court and how the case came up to this court and the asserted errors.

The statement of the *issues* is simply an indication of the precise points the court passed on in deciding the case. Formulating them in express terms helps to distinguish between what the court *held* and what it said merely by way of *dictum*.

Although the court's argument usually appears before its decision in the opinion, your brief will be clearer and you will be in a better position to discuss the case if you state the decision on the issues first and follow that with a statement of the reasons for it. Above all, don't confuse the two. Don't just state a general proposition of law as the

court's _decision_. Indicate *how the controversy was settled,* and then put down the arguments and propositions of law relied upon
as reasons for that settlement in light of the
facts of the case.

To help you visualize the matters just discussed about reading and briefing cases, here
is an opinion from the Minnesota Supreme
Court, edited and printed as you might find
it in your casebook for the course in Tort
law. Following that is a "brief" of the case
which illustrates the way in which the case
might be suitably abstracted:

GERMOLUS v. SAUSSER

Supreme Court of Minnesota, 1901.
83 Minn. 141, 85 N.W. 946.

START, C. J. Action to recover damages
for personal injuries sustained by the plaintiff by reason of an assault and battery per-
petrated upon him November 14, 1899, by
the defendant. The defense was that the act
was done in self-defense. Verdict for plaintiff for $1,100, and the defendant appealed
from an order denying his motion for a new
trial.

All of the assignments of error, which are
well assigned, relate to exceptions to the

charge of the trial court to the jury. The evidence on the part of the plaintiff tended to show that the defendant made an unprovoked assault upon him, and struck him over the head with the heavy end of a whip stock, whereby the plaintiff was knocked senseless, and sustained serious injuries. The evidence also tends to show that there had been some words between the parties growing out of the fact that the plaintiff, who had been ploughing a field lying along the highway, had ploughed within the limits of the highway. The plaintiff had stopped his team, and was standing by the side of his plough, some ten rods from the highway, when the defendant struck him. The defendant's own testimony was to this effect:

"He (plaintiff) was ploughing and when he saw me driving on the highway he stopped his team, and called to me to come over, and repeated the call seven or eight times. I stopped my team, and asked him what he wanted. He said, 'Come over this way.' I got off the wagon, took my coat off, as it was too heavy (this was November 21st), and went over to the plaintiff, and asked him what he was calling to me for; and he swung his whip around hitting me on the arm, and I jerked it out of his hand, and hit him with

[*55*]

it, and then he let himself drop. I had to hit him to protect myself. I had the whip near the stock, and I swung it over and gave it to him." * * *

The trial court gave to the jury, with others, the instructions following:

"Now, in this case, you are to consider, in the first place, whether any element of self-defense enters into it. According to the testimony of the defendant himself, even if that were true, that the plaintiff struck at him with a whip stock, was it then necessary for him, to defend himself, to jerk it out of the plaintiff's hands, and then strike the plaintiff with it? He was only justified in doing that if it was necessary for his own protection, in his own self-defense."

"There is no full defense made out in this case, unless the defendant has established by a preponderance of the evidence that the battery committed upon the plaintiff, as admitted, was necessary for his own self-protection, and to prevent the plaintiff from further battering him."

It is the contention of the defendant that the first two instructions given were erroneous, in that they, in effect, made his right of self-defense depend upon an actual necessity for the use of force in order to protect himself, instead of upon the then apparent necessity of the situation, and withdrew from the jury the consideration of the question whether at the time the defendant entertained an honest and reasonable belief that it was necessary to use the force which he did use in order to protect himself.

The rule as to self-defense is the same in civil and criminal actions. The rule is this: An act, otherwise criminal, is justifiable when it is done to protect the person committing it, or another whom he is bound to protect, from imminent personal injury, the act appearing reasonably necessary to prevent the injury, nothing more being done than is reasonably necessary. G.S.1894, Sec. 6308. This does not require that the necessity for doing the act must be actual; for it is sufficient if there is either a real or apparent necessity for so doing.

But the mere belief of a person that it is necessary to use force to prevent an injury to himself is not alone sufficient to make out a case of self-defense, for the facts as they appear to him at the time must be such as reasonably to justify such belief.

It follows that the instructions in this case were not strictly accurate, but the error was without prejudice; for, upon the defendant's own testimony, we hold as a matter of law that he was not justified in beating the plaintiff. To hold otherwise would be a reproach to the administration of justice; for, accepting the defendant's own statement of what occurred, there was neither a real nor an apparent necessity for knocking the plaintiff down after he had been disarmed. Nor were the facts, viewed from any standpoint, such as reasonably to justify the defendant in believing that there was any such necessity.

. .

Order affirmed.

. . . .

(SAMPLE BRIEF)

Casebook, page ——. Germolus v. Sausser, 83 Minn. 141, 85 N.W. 946 (1901).

Facts:

Action for damages for an alleged assault and battery. Def. claimed he acted in self-defense. Pl's evidence was that Def. struck him with a whip without provocation. Def's evidence was that Pl. first struck him on the arm with the whip and that he then jerked the whip out of Pl's hand and struck Pl. with the butt end of it to protect himself. The court instructed the jury, in substance, that they would first have to find that there was some element of self-defense present, and that even if they found that Pl. first struck Def. that would be no legal justification for Def's act unless they further found that it "was necessary" for Def. to strike Pl. to prevent Pl. from further attacking him. Def. excepted to this instruction. Verdict for Pl. Def. moved for a new trial claiming that the instruction to the jury was erroneous because it made his right of self-defense depend on the actual necessity rather than on his reasonable belief as to the necessity of self-defense. Motion denied, and Def. appealed from the order denying his motion.

Issues:

(1) Whether instructions correct as to self-defense—whether actual necessity is the test.

(2) Whether, if not, the facts justified a verdict for Def. under the correct rule of law.

Decision: No, as to both issues. Order Affirmed.

Reasons:

(1) An act, otherwise criminal, is justifiable when done to protect the actor from imminent personal injury so long as it appears reasonably necessary to prevent the injury and so long as it does not go beyond what appears to be reasonably necessary. It is not required that the necessity for doing the act be actual. Reasonable belief is sufficient. The rule as to self-defense in criminal actions applies in civil actions. The instructions were thus not accurate.

(2) Def's own testimony, however, shows no real or apparent necessity for beating Pl. after he was disarmed. The facts are so clear that it can be held as a matter of law that there was no justification for Def's act. Thus the erroneous instructions were not prejudicial.

* * * *

d. "Canned Briefs."

You'll no doubt be told that you can save yourself the trouble of reading and briefing the cases in your casebooks by using ready-made abstracts or "canned briefs" of them prepared by someone else. Don't be a sucker and fall for this. It's not true. Canned briefs may sometimes enable you to "get by" in class and fool the professor into thinking you are prepared when you aren't, but if that's your object in law school you simply aren't interested in being a lawyer. The first step toward being a good lawyer is learning how to read and analyze a case properly, and you can't learn that simply by reading someone else's brief, even if it's a good one. Proper case reading and analysis is as fundamental to law practice as proper blocking and tackling are to football, and to learn how to do it you've got to study the cases themselves, see exactly what the judges have said about the facts of each controversy and the rules and principles applicable to it, and how they went about deciding it. When you go out into practice you'll have to read and analyze the cases for yourself—you won't have any "canned briefs" to rely on—so why not learn how right away? And, if you're going to read the cases yourself, why bother with canned briefs? The only reason for briefing cases, aside from their incidental value as memoranda, is the benefit you derive from making them—the help they give you in reading the cases more carefully and thoroughly. You can't derive that benefit by buying or acquiring them ready-made. Don't be fooled by someone whose main reason for interesting you in this "something-for-nothing" idea is more than likely a desire to make some extra money. There just isn't any short-cut by which you can learn law without putting in a good many hours of plain hard study and reading.

SECTION 4. CLASSWORK — TAKING NOTES — CLASS ATTENDANCE

a. Teaching Methods

Class procedure under the case method varies considerably, depending upon the particular instructor. In many courses the instructor employs mainly a *Socratic* method of teaching, asking students for statements of the cases and then asking questions about them, posing hypothetical problems, challenging the students' answers, getting several students involved in the arguments and largely leaving for student determination the conclusions to be drawn from the cases. In a few courses, however, the instructor may spend much of the time lecturing. In many others there will be some questioning and student discussion coupled with short lectures or summaries by the instructor. No matter what the instructional system is, the objective

[62]

is the same, namely, to supplement and integrate your case reading and individual study.

Class work affords you the opportunity to analyze critically and compare the cases you have read so as to determine their value as precedents more accurately. It furnishes information about other cases. In short, it helps you tie up the individual cases, fill in the gaps and get a better understanding of the rules and legal policies applicable to various related types of legal problems and controversies in each area of law.

Since a substantial amount of class discussion is expected and encouraged by most instructors, and since it stimulates more active and critical thinking about the cases, problems, rules, etc., it is important to participate in it as much as is feasible in view of the size of the class.

b. Taking Notes

It's absolutely essential that you take notes in class unless you have a memory that never fades. The courses are relatively long, you are studying a number of them at the same time, and it's almost impossible to review adequately for your law school and bar exams unless you have a good set of notes in each course. Notetaking of course, is not standardized. It's largely an individual problem, and each of you will have to work out the details of your own system. The object is to take the sort of notes that will be most helpful to *you*, and although there are no ironclad rules, the following suggestions should be helpful.

In the first place, *don't try to write down everything that is said in class*! Someone defined a lecture as being "a process by which the lecturer's notes become the student's notes without going through the minds of either", and that is exactly what it is when you simply write down everything you hear. Pick out the *important* things—especially the *questions* asked by the instructor, the *hypothetical problems* he poses, the *reasons* for various rules, the policies involved and explanations that you really want to remember —and let the rest go! For example: when you're starting a new Chapter or sub-division in your casebook, write the title or the subtitle in your notebook. If the instructor makes any general statements about the Chapter or sub-division, write a brief summary of them in your own words. That orients you for the things to come.

When you come to a discussion of an assigned case, write down its name and *then stop and listen to what is being said about it.* Presumably you've read and briefed it, so compare what you hear with your own impressions and understanding of the case. Think about the *questions* that are asked and the answers given to them. If you disagree with what is said, or don't understand it, speak up as soon as there is an opportunity.

When a hypothetical problem is suggested take it down if you can, but don't lose the thread of the discussion. If the instructor makes some statement or explanation during the discussion of a case that seems to you to be important and worth remembering, summarize it. Weigh his statements carefully and separate the grain from the chaff. Finally, when the discussion has proceeded to a point where a conclusion has been reached or a rule developed, get it clearly in mind and then write a concise, accurate statement of it *in your own words* together with any explanation of it you think is necessary. *Remember that the reasons for the rules are often more important than the rules themselves.* Don't be too sketchy, however. Write complete sentences so that when you come to read your notes later on they'll be clear and understandable. Take down all citations to other cases, texts and law review material, and if the instructor is obviously *dictating* some quotation or statement try to copy it. If he thinks it's important enough to dictate, it's important enough to take down.

When you go from one problem to the next, indicate the transition. Try to make your notes a condensed text, running along smoothly and weaving the cases together without puzzling gaps or a lot of irrelevant or redundant statements. Your whole objective in taking notes is to get a permanent, understandable and accurate record of the *questions raised* and the *important* things said in class about the cases and the rules, policies and principles of law they exemplify. To accomplish this you have to concentrate all of the time and follow everything closely. Try not to let your attention wander when the questions, comments or discussion seems unimportant or repetitive. You may miss an important aspect of the problem or case under discussion.

c. Class Attendance and Importance

The reason for having formal classes, particularly in first-year and other basic law school courses, is not just to give the instructor an opportunity to lecture or demonstrate his brilliance but to *add depth and dimension to your understanding of what you read and study*. The object is to give you background for the cases, raise questions, develop insights, point out conflicts and comparisons, and suggest relationships that you cannot get just from studying the material yourself. The instructor can bring these out because of his experience, training and specialized study of the subject. His job in class is to help you get a broader, deeper and more meaningful understanding of the materials. If he does not do that he is not doing what he is supposed to do. If he does his job adequately it's obvious that when you do not attend class you are missing an important ingredient in the mix from which you can derive the necessary high professional level of your legal education.

Just from the standpoint of your own self-interest, and without regard to whether attendance is required, it is important not to miss a class unless you are ill or otherwise unable to be there. When you do have to miss a class session, get the notes of someone who has attended (and who takes good, legible notes) and copy or summarize them in your own notebook to maintain the continuity when you review the subject.

It is true, of course, that a person with good legal aptitudes can get a fair understanding of a legal subject just from intensive reading and study of a good casebook or textbook and the statutes and other materials cited in them. Prior to the present century most lawyers in this country got their legal training, and became qualified for admission to the bar, by working for several years as an apprentice in an established lawyer's office and "reading law" in the reported cases and from standard treatises and texts like those of Blackstone, Kent, Story and other distinguished judges and legal scholars. A number of first-rate lawyers were trained in this manner but, by-and-large, this type of legal education varied greatly in quality and balance, was largely hit-and-miss, and tended to produce narrow, shallow and mechanical lawyers with little intellectual depth or professional grasp of the function of law and lawyers in society. Their clients and the public, of course, paid the price of such professional mediocrity.

Since about 1870 it has been increasingly recognized that to fulfill adequately their professional functions lawyers should have both a background of liberal arts college education and also three or four years of organized intensive legal education in the major areas of law, presented by skilled, professional law teachers in properly accredited law schools requiring an adequate, professional level of student-achievement for graduation and a degree. Such education and degree, plus satisfactory performance on tough, comprehensive bar-exams, are now required for admission to the bar in most if not all of our states to insure the public of at least minimum professional competence in their lawyers.

It has also been recognized that to provide the necessary professional level and intensity of law study, law schools and teachers should provide not only good casebooks, textbooks and a prescribed course of reading in them for their students in each basic subject but also an adequate number of formal classes in each, conducted by a teacher-specialist, for intensive discussion and elaboration of the study material. As a result, the two law-school accrediting organizations—the Association of American Law Schools and the Section on Legal Education of the American Bar Association—require that an approved law school must, for its professional degree, require a prescribed number of credit hours of *study in residence* by its students. Such required *residence-study* has reference to the *class-hours* devoted to the courses and presupposes regular class attendance in addition to out-of-class study and preparation.

Because of its importance many law schools *require* class attendance and penalize excessive unexcused absences, but even where that is not formally prescribed, regular class attendance is expected. The reasons are quite obvious in view of the functions and importance of class work.

There are, of course, some courses such as Legal Writing, Appellate Advocacy and Trial Practice, plus advanced seminars and clinical programs, in which students do most of the work outside of class and in which class meetings are less structured and sometimes infrequent. Generally, however, regular class attendance and participation in properly-taught basic courses is indispensable to a *good* legal education.

SECTION 5. SUPPLEMENTARY READING

Sometimes your instructor will assign for study certain cases, statutes or other material not reproduced in the casebook. Also, you will find in the casebook extensive references to additional cases in the reports, law review articles and comments, annotations to leading cases, pertinent discussion in law treatises and textbooks, law digests and encyclopedias, the Restatements, and other sources of legal information. Of course you will not be expected to read and digest all of this cited material, at least when it's not specially assigned. It is made available to you as a supplement to the required material and a source of further information about questions not dealt with thoroughly or developed at all in the casebook material.

The important thing is to use it intelligently. Don't disregard it entirely simply because it's not specifically assigned. On the other hand don't gorge yourself by reading so much of it that you simply get fuddled and confused. Dip into it whenever you feel uncertain about a problem, or when your knowledge of some phase of a course is sketchy and incomplete. In using it, remember that your required reading, classwork and review comes first. It's the foundation on which you build, so don't neglect it in order to do extensive outside reading about something you won't understand without it. Outside reading is an *accessory,* to be used in filling in the chinks and in clarifying the unclear.

Don't try to do much supplementary reading the first few months in law school. Wait until you get the hang of things and learn the vocabulary. Then acquire the habit of looking in this outside material for the answers to your questions before running to your instructor. You'll need that habit after you leave school and have nothing but the books to go to for help. Intelligent use of other law books is the principal device by which you gradually become self reliant and mentally independent of a teacher.

In addition to the strictly technical law books, there are a number of treatises on the broader aspects of the legal system. These you should explore to some extent simply for the cultural background they will give you. A lawyer is more than a legal craftsman. His work, in its broadest aspects, is really social engineering. He should have an understanding of the place of law in society and its function as an instrument of social order. Such classics as Pollock and Maitland's History of English Law, Holdsworth's History of English Law, Wigmore's Panorama of the World's Legal Systems, Burdick's

Bench and Bar of Other Lands, Holmes' Lectures on the Common Law, Cardozo's Nature of the Judicial Process and others are worth some exploration.

SECTION 6. USING STUDENT TEXTBOOKS AND "HORNBOOKS"

A student textbook or "Hornbook" is a concise, one-volume treatise covering the main areas in a particular legal subject (Torts, Contracts, Criminal Law, etc.). It does not attempt to deal with all aspects of the subject or present extensive citations or analyses, as do the major, multi-volume reference treatises (e. g. Corbin on Contracts, Wigmore on Evidence, American Law of Property, etc.). Some student textbooks are one-volume condensations and abridgements of major treatises but most are not. Some are excellent, many are good and some are either superficial or not particularly well-written.

Student textbooks are normally written by legal scholars who have specialized in the subjects covered and have spent years studying and writing law review articles or books about the cases, statutes and problems involved. The textbook is an attempt by the author to state and explain in a logical and systematic way the legal rules, policies and principles that the courts or other judicial or quasi-judicial tribunals have applied in deciding various types of cases in that field. The text concentrates on general rules, conclusions and generalizations, summarizes the reasons for these and cites the leading cases, law review discussions and sometimes the collected-case annotations where many cases are discussed. Textbooks are *rule*-oriented rather than *problem*-oriented, representing the author's considered opinions and conclusions as to *what he believes the law is* on various points.

When reading any law treatise—whether major treatise or student textbook—remember that you are dealing with condensed, concentrated material. The holdings in dozens of cases frequently are distilled into a single sentence or paragraph. Conflicting groups of decisions and rules may be summarized in a page or less. In student textbooks reasons for the rules, the policies involved and the arguments pro and con on debatable questions usually are stated quite briefly with only the leading cases discussed in any detail. This type of writing must be read and re-read carefully and with a conscious effort to keep in mind the *specific fact situations* to which the rules and generalizations apply. Don't try to *skim* through a textbook!

Keep in mind, also, that the statements in the text are *not* official, authoritative legal pronouncements like statutes or court opinions. They are simply the author's conclusions and generalizations as to what he believes the law is on the basis of his extensive study and analysis of the cases and statutes. His statements are usually quite accurate but they inevitably involve *his* interpretation of what the courts and legislatures *meant* by their pronouncements, not *theirs*, and are thus not binding on them. Textbooks are therefore *secondary*, not primary, sources of law and must, as a consequence be read critically and not simply accepted as the final word on the subject.

Don't try to use a student textbook as a *substitute* for your casebook in a law school course. Students sometimes think they can avoid the hard, grubby work of reading, analyzing and briefing cases and learn "The Law" adequately from a textbook. The difficulty with this is that the straight textbook does not exemplify how courts *use* rules in actually deciding cases—how they *interpret* statutes and prior decisions, draw factual distinctions between cases, analyze the facts of the case before them, and decide *which* prior decisions, rules or statutory provisions should properly apply to those facts. The case opinions reflect what courts have actually decided in specific controversies and their explanations of their decisions. Court opinions illustrate how lawyers and judges *apply* rules and precedents. A textbook merely states the author's generalizations and interpretations of what the courts have *held* and *said* as to the law.

A good textual discussion of the law on a subject, of course, can be a very helpful *supplement* in evaluating the cases you've studied if it has been written by a thorough, competent scholar. That is why the authors of many of the newer casebooks insert in them quite a few of their own textual commentaries on the problems involved in or related to the cases. In fact, some course books contain so much text that they are actually combination casebook-textbooks.

A separate student textbook by another author, however, may be quite useful when you come to review your case-briefs and notes. If, after reviewing, you still feel that you don't have a very good understanding of some problem, the discussion of it in a textbook gives you the point of view of another scholar which you can compare with your own impressions of the cases and the observations of your instructor. A textbook may bring out aspects of the problems that had not occurred to you and thus may clarify your understanding. However, it is not imperative that you use textbooks in reviewing unless they are assigned for study. They normally are simply a source of assistance if you feel that you need it. It is also not essential that you buy one unless the instructor requires it for supplementary study. But the really good ones can be kept as part of your own law library and are worth purchasing if you can afford it.

Another way in which good student textbooks may be helpful to you is in subjects in which you do not take a course in school. It is not possible to take all of the courses offered in the curriculum during the normal period spent in law school. In some areas, like Agency, Partnership, Damages, Suretyship, Insurance, and other well-developed fields of law which may be included on the bar exam, there are good textbooks and you can get a fair general understanding of the basic principles and rules without a formal course by studying a textbook during a vacation period. This does not give you as effective learning as taking a formal course from a good instructor and casebook but it can help you get some understanding of less difficult subjects and enable you to take more courses in the difficult subjects where an instructor's guidance and intensive case study or research are essential.

SECTION 7. REVIEW

Under any method of law study and especially under the case method, proper and systematic review is as indispensable as proper case reading or text reading or classwork. Nevertheless, most beginning law students are inclined to regard reviewing with distaste. By and large it is the most neglected and poorly done part of their work. They tend to think of it as nothing but a tedious process of memorization, accomplished by simply going over and over their material until they know it by heart. This is probably due to the fact that in elementary and high school courses, and to some extent in prelegal college courses, the emphasis is mainly on the student's ability to *remember* what he has studied rather than on his ability to *analyze and use it*. As we have seen, the main object of law study is to learn how to *use* and *apply* the cases, rules and principles studied, and it is mainly through intelligent review that this object is accomplished. Review is the assembly line and finishing process in your mental factory. It is the process by which you gather the mass of details picked up in each day's study and mold them into a coherent, usable piece of mental equipment. If you really understand its function and how it should be done, reviewing becomes one of the most interesting and constructive parts of your work.

There are two general types of review—*day-to-day* review and *periodic* review—and it is essential that you do both types. Since each serves a somewhat distinct function they will be separately treated.

a. Day-to-Day Review

The object and purpose of day-to-day review is quite apparent from its name. It is primarily a device for "nailing down" or clinching the material you study as you go along—for fixing more firmly in your mind the important propositions developed in each course from day to day. In addition, of course, it helps you tie up each day's work in the course with that of the previous day and eliminate errors, omissions and confusion in your notes. By doing it regularly, you thoroughly assimilate the essential material and at the same time smooth out each course and keep it from becoming a succession of blobs and gaps.

As to the most effective method of doing this type of review, there is obviously no uniform rule. A system that works well for some may not be particularly effective for others, and in the last analysis you have to work out the program that gives *you* the best results.

Some students prefer to go over and edit their class notes as soon after class as a study period is available. Others prefer to wait until they are ready to prepare for the next class hour. At either point they read carefully the previous five or six pages of class notes taken in that course, including the briefs of the cases to which they refer, reading critically and editing their notes as they go along, completing unfinished sentences, crossing out irrelevant or inconsequential matter, adding further statements or explanations that now seem necessary and underlining the most important rules and explanations.

Under either method of day-to-day review it is important to check up on inconsistencies and statements that seem wrong, and make sure you *understand* those that are right. By doing this you put your notes in better shape, catch errors and omissions before the subject has grown too cold, and get a better understanding of the material covered. This is also the best time to read any collateral matter that has been suggested.

Unless you have just completed a chapter or division in the casebook, the cases you are about to study for the next day carry on from where you left off, and you'll have a much easier time reading and understanding them with the previous work fresh in your mind. On the average it shouldn't take more than fifteen or twenty minutes per course to do this brief reviewing, and in view of the fact that it warms up your mental motor so that you shift into your advance reading without the delay usually encountered in trying to "get in the mood" for studying, there is very little increase in your total studying time when you review just before you read the next cases. Furthermore, you are maintaining the all important *continuity* in each course by this daily "doubling back" even though you are taking several courses contemporaneously and are making abrupt shifts from one to the other several times a day.

b. Periodic Review

The object and purpose of periodic review is to get a broad mental picture of the *main divisions* in each course and, ultimately, of the whole course. In studying law you are considering something more than a formless mass of specific legal problems with rules and solutions to match. You are dealing with an elaborate and complicated *system of classification* in which the whole mass has been divided into a number of major categories or divisions which, in turn, have been divided and sub-divided in considerable detail. These divisions and classifications have been made for various purposes and from various points of view. For example, there are the very broad classifications of substantive law, remedial law and procedural law; public law and private law. Within these are other classifications such as Property, Contracts, Torts, Criminal Law and so on. These classifications or categories, of course, are not watertight compartments. They overlap to a considerable extent and are highly interrelated. Nevertheless, they make possible the systematic study and practice of law by breaking up the whole mass of legal problems into groups and sub-groups of more or less similar problems which can be dealt with and studied as units because they have certain common factors and elements.

Each course in law school deals with one or more of the larger categories or divisions within the whole field of law. It comprehends a general *type* of problem—a broad group of problems having something in common and to which broad general principles can be applied. Thus, for example, the course in Contracts, looking at it as a whole, is tied together by the fact that all the problems with which it deals have to do with *promises* and *agreements* between various persons. Within this larger category of Contracts, of course, there are a number of major sub-divisions, such as Mutual Assent, Consideration, Conditions, Performance, etc.; and within each of these major subdivisions there are further sub-classes and groupings down to the specific, individual problems.

In your day-to-day study and review, your attention is focused primarily on individual cases and small groups of cases dealing first with one specific problem and then another. It is essential, of course, that you understand these problems and the rules applicable to them, but it is difficult if not impossible to get any perspective and see the broader groupings and larger outlines of the whole course from the daily plodding alone. The impression you usually get is that the course is just a succession of relatively unrelated details, and as long as that impression remains and your legal knowledge stays in that undigested form it is not very *usable* in helping you *solve new problems*. If, for example, you encounter a new set of facts in an exam or in practice, and you have nothing in your mind but a mass of unrelated specific cases and statutes, it is sheer luck if you manage to find the ones that fit the new problem and help you solve it. If, on the other hand, you understand the main classifications in the law, the principal subdivisions within them, the further classes and sub-classes, and the interrelations and overlappings, you have a mental map or chart of the whole field by means of which you can quickly *classify* your problem and thus make your way back to the specific cases and rules which dealt with *that type of problem*.

The details you have learned in each course must be put together and tied up into a coherent whole. You must get far enough back from the individual trees to see the whole forest. The device by which you accomplish that is periodic review, and in doing periodic reviewing that is your primary objective. Keep constantly in mind the fact that you are not merely *memorizing* the material you have studied. You have already spent a good many hours on the details, first when you read and briefed the cases, then in class, and again in your daily review. If you don't understand them after all that work, there's nothing much you can do about it. The thing you are now looking for is the *connection* between all the individual problems and rules— the *central theme* of the various chapters and the *broad general principles, policies and reasoning* on which the specific rules are based.

Effective periodic review in any particular course must necessarily be done only at relatively infrequent intervals, since the object is to get a broad view of the larger segments of the course. Some people recommend that this type of review be done at regular intervals, that is, every two, three or four weeks in each course. A more logical system, however, would seem to be to do it at the end of each *chapter* or *main division* of the casebook. The chapters and main divisions in the casebooks mark off the principal categories or groups of problems in each particular field, and are therefore suitable large units for consideration when you are trying to put details together in a coherent whole. You probably will not be finishing chapters at the same time in every course, and therefore your periodic review will not often pile up or be an undue burden. Comprehensive reviewing, of course, must also be done in preparing for exams.

As to the specific method or procedure to be followed in doing periodic and pre-exam review, there is no uniform rule. The most important thing is to keep in mind the objective outlined above. Start in by considering the whole chapter or division *as a whole*. Look back over all the cases considered and pick out the similarities and common elements. Regard each specific case as an example of a *general type* of problem. Then pick out the various smaller *groups* of specific problems within the larger group.

Try to formulate broad general principles and policies of law applicable to the whole group, and then work out the general rules, exceptions and qualifications that are applied in the subsidiary groups. For example, if you are reviewing a chapter in Contracts dealing with Offers, notice first that all the cases and problems deal with the general type of situation in which one person proposes a bargain-agreement of some sort to another person. Then observe that this broad group is divided into unilateral and bilateral proposals—those contemplating an act and those contemplating a counter promise in return by the offeree. Within these main subdivisions, single out the smaller groupings such as offers in auctions, commercial sales, services and the like, as well as groupings dealing with the duration, revocation and interpretation of the various sorts of offers. With this structural picture in mind, pick out such general principles and rules as the one that "an offer not limited in time lasts only for a reasonable time;" or that "an offer is to be interpreted from the standpoint of the reasonable offeree." Of course, these are merely suggestions, but they may help you in getting the idea and formulating your own system of periodic review.

c. Reviewing With Other Students—Discussions and Arguments

Some students prefer to work alone in reviewing. Many, however, find it helpful to review with one or more classmates. Sometimes each will first read his or her notes and briefs and then get together for a "rap" or "bull" session about the cases and problems, arguing the pros and cons; and clarifying points on which there is misunderstanding. Sometimes two or three will simply get together and take turns summarizing portions of the material, discussing points of disagreement and arguing over disputed questions. Getting others' points of view can be helpful in clarifying one's own understanding of a problem, and arguing debatable rules, policies and problem-solutions is good training for the advocacy functions that lawyers must perform in representing clients in legal proceedings under our adversary system.

A lawyer normally has no choice as to which party he or she will represent in a legal controversy. Lawyers cannot properly solicit clients. The client must come to the lawyer who, if the client is accepted, must argue that client's position. Lawyers who work in the legal department of a corporation or some governmental body must represent its side of the controversies in which it becomes involved. Learning how to formulate the arguments *on each side* of any debatable question is an important part of legal training. Arguing legal problems with one's classmates in law school is good practice for this aspect of the lawyer's job.

SECTION 8. OUTLINES

Making written outlines of each course is extremely helpful when doing your periodic and pre-exam reviewing. It not only gives you a tangible picture of the organization of the course, but also compels you to do the reviewing more thoroughly, carefully and systematically. In many schools you will find printed or mimeographed outlines of the various courses offered for sale by enterprising upperclassmen or graduates. If these happen to be good outlines, which they frequently are *not*, they will be of some help to you by indicating the broad divisions and subdivisions of the course, and by indicating the general rules and principles of law. However, you can get most of that sort of help free from the table of contents in your casebook or a text on the subject with much less chance of being misled. Furthermore, the real value of a written outline lies in making it yourself—in combing through your material and organizing it in a systematic way so you can put it down in outline form.

In making your outlines there are a number of things to keep in mind. First of all, remember that they are not merely a condensation of your notes. Their main purpose is to bring out in written form, clearly and sharply, the *organization* of each course so that you can more clearly see its principal divisions and subdivisions. Outlines embody the things you look for and dig out in your periodic review, whereas your notebooks embody the details you learn in your day-to-day study. The outline should emphasize, as its name suggests, the skeleton or framework of the course. Your notes and cases are the flesh and blood, and you should not put so many details from them into the outline that they conceal the framework. Put in just enough of the general rules, exceptions and qualifications to integrate the outline with the notebook. It is all right to insert page references or names of important cases, but don't overdo it. Keep the outline an *outline*.

A good starting point, both for periodic review and for making an outline in each course, is the table of contents of your casebook. It gives you a concise picture of the way the whole course is organized—the main divisions, chapters and sections—together with some indication of the content of each. In some courses you can use the table of contents as written, and simply fill it in with such further statements, rules and references as are necessary. In other courses you may want to rearrange the various topics and groups of problems to some extent. Sometimes, where the table of contents is not particularly detailed and merely gives chapter titles, you will have to work out the subdivisions within the chapters from the material in them. For example, in some casebooks on Agency you will find a chapter entitled "Duties of Agent to Principal" without any subdivisions indicated. There are divisions within it, however, and in reviewing the material dealt with, you would make some such outline as the following:

Chapter ——. Duties Of Agent To Principal.

Deals generally with the legal obligations of an agent to his principal—servant to his master—in various situations.

A. General Duty of All Agents to Act for the Best Interests of the Principal and to Exercise Reasonable Skill, Care and Diligence to Protect and Advance Them.

　1. Agent liable to principal if negligent in his work. (See NB (notebook) page ——.)

> 2. Agent only liable for damages caused by his negligence. (NB ——.)
>
> 3. Breach of duty may warrant his discharge. (NB ——.)

B. Duty to Sustantially Perform His Contract with the Principal if There is One.

Parties may make any agreement they wish that is not illegal, immoral or against public policy. Their relation is consensual and they must live up to the terms of their contract if valid according to contract law. (NB ——.)

C. General Duty of All Agents to Follow Principal's Lawful Instructions and to Obey Reasonable Orders.

It is the principal's business—he has right to say how it shall be run within reasonable and legal limitations.

> 1. Reasonableness is question of fact in each case. (NB ——).
>
> 2. Orders may be violated in emergency. (NB ——.)

D. Duty of Loyalty—Negative Obligation—Requires Agent to Refrain from any Conduct which Might Jeopardize the Principal's Interests.

Is a duty arising out of the fiduciary character of the agency relation—May be modified by principal's consent.

> 1. Prohibits agent from acting as adverse party (buyer-seller) **or for**

adverse party without principal's consent. (NB ——.)

2. Prohibits agent from competing with principal. (NB ——.)

3. Prohibits agent from making secret profits. (NB ——.)

4. Prohibits agent from intentionally disclosing principal's business secrets or using them for his own advantage without principal's consent. (NB ——.)

5. Principal has numerous remedies for breach of this duty—Discharge—Forfeiture of agent's compensation —Action for damages—Bill to enforce constructive trust—etc. (NB ——.)

E. General Duty to Account to Principal for Money or Things Received for or from Him—Duty to Pay Over to Principal When Required.

Duty based on theory that money or property received by agent in course of employment belongs to principal and must be accounted for. (NB ——.)

1. Qualifications on duty in case of money or property tainted by illegal or immoral transaction. (NB ——.)

2. Remedies of principal—action for accounting—constructive trust—etc. (NB ——.)

The above outline is, of course, merely illustrative. You might make it more elaborate with a larger number of groupings and the names of cases. You might arrange the subdivisions in a different order. You might wish to make more specific references to the material in your NB (notebook) rather than the simple page reference. As it stands, however, it brings out the salient points of the chapter—the main principles involved—and exemplifies the essential skeletonized, analytical nature of an outline.

One big advantage of making such outlines is that they greatly facilitate exam writing and problem solving in general. By organizing the material in each course and then lifting out the framework in the form of a short, compact outline, you have created a picture that can be easily memorized and carried with you into the examination room and later out into practice. It is the sort of picture you will be able to recall long after the details of the course have faded out, and by mental reference to it you can quickly classify a new problem and "see the points involved in it" without the necessity of culling a mass of irrelevant material. True, you can get this same mental picture or catalogue by careful periodic review without making a written outline, but there is something about putting it down in black and white that brings it out sharply and makes it stick.

Perhaps this discussion of outlines and periodic review is overly long and detailed, but this phase of your study is so essential, and at the same time so frequently misunderstood or omitted entirely, that it deserves special emphasis.

SECTION 9. STUDYING FOR EXAMS

In preparation for taking law exams it is essential that you first thoroughly *review* all of your briefs and notes in each course on the material to be covered by the exam. If it is a *final* exam this means reviewing the whole course and completing your outline of it.

Actually no special type of reviewing or outlining for exams is necessary. What has been explained above in Section 7b. about periodic review is equally applicable to over-all review at the end of a course or segment. The purposes and objectives are the same: to put the material together systematically in a unified whole so as to get the broad picture of the subject and see the parts in relation to the whole. Making a good, analytical outline not only helps materially in doing this but also gives you a concise, schematic pic-

ture of the course—its main divisions, subdivisions and sub-subdivisions—which is easy
to memorize and use during the exam as a basis for classifying each exam problem and determining the possible issues and sub-issues
that may be involved in it. Having a good,
skeletonized mental outline of the types of
problem covered in a course is like having a
good catalog or index by which you can determine which particular cases and statutes
among those you've studied and discussed
may be applicable to the exam problem
you're analyzing. After reading the problem
and the question(s) asked about it you can
run through your mental outline and determine which parts of the course apply to the
problem and where it fits into the course.

When you've mastered the techniques of
proper periodic review and outlining, you've
learned how to *study* for exams. After completing your review and outline it is usually
helpful, if you have the time, to go over old
exam questions in each subject to see what
kinds of problems are used in it. Also, in preparing for your first-year exams it is helpful
to study some answers that have been written to such exam problems. In Part II of
this book, following the explanation of the
nature and purposes of problem-questions in

law exams, and how to go about analyzing and writing proper answers, there are many pages devoted to illustrative exam problems, one or more for each of the usual first-year law courses, with a good "A" answer and a not-so-good marginal answer to each for purpose of comparison.

These sample problems have been selected, edited, and included to give you illustrations of various types of exam problems you might encounter. These were prepared by a number of instructors in first-year courses and actually used in their law school exams. The samples of what they regarded as good and marginal answers to each will give you a general idea of what sort of answers they received, how these were evaluated, and what will be expected from you in your answers.

Thus, after you have finished reviewing and outlining for each course (and have studied the general explanation of law exams in the first part of Part II of this book) turn to the sample problems and answers on that subject in Part II. Read each problem carefully and the question(s) it asks. Analyze it thoroughly and consider how you would answer the question(s) on the basis of your study. Then read carefully the Good "A"

Answer and the Marginal Answer and the "Comment" thereon, comparing the answers with your own conclusion as to how you would have answered the question(s). This should give you a definite idea of how an answer should and should not be written.

Also, in most law schools there is an available collection or file of exam problems previously given in its courses by various instructors for use by the students in preparing for their current exams. Reading some of these can give you considerable insight into the specific kinds of problems commonly used by the teachers in your own school in their courses. To test and develop your own skill in analyzing exam problems and writing appropriate answers you will probably find it helpful, after your reviewing and outlining, to select one of these prior-year problems, allot yourself the prescribed time for answering it and then go through the process of analyzing it and ascertaining and organizing the issues to be discussed and then actually writing an answer to it. Try to follow the suggestions for this in Part II, Section 1d, of this book (pages 118–129, below) and see what kind of answer you produce. Perhaps a classmate whose ability you respect will join you in doing this so that you can each read and offer a critique of the other's answer and discuss the shortcomings in your answers. There is definitely a skill and technique involved in effectively writing answers to these law exam problems, just as there is in other types of legal writing, and the best way to develop it is to practice doing it in preparation for your first-year exams. Many schools give practice exams to help you in this effort but you won't be wasting time in doing some additional work to develop your own "examsmanship".

When you come to review for the bar exams it is also helpful to get copies of old bar exams, if they're available, and study the problems to see how, if at all, they differ from those you've answered in law school.

•

PART II

LAW EXAM PROBLEMS, ANSWERS AND COMMENTS

INTRODUCTION TO PART II

This part of the book attempts to explain and illustrate problem-type law exams and how to write appropriate answers to them.

The first section contains an analysis of the principal objectives and types of examinations; the reasons for using problem-questions in law exams; what the examiner looks for in the answers to law exam problems; and effective procedures to follow in analyzing them and planning, organizing and writing the answers.

The second section contains a number of carefully selected, illustrative problem-questions from exams in the traditional first-year law courses with samples of good and marginal answers to each and comments thereon. These are intended to show first-year law students what sort of problems they may encounter in each of their exams, how such problems have been answered and the ingredients of a good answer. Studying these

in reviewing and preparing for exams should
be helpful in learning how to write appropriate answers to law problem-questions.

SECTION 1.   EXAMINATION   OBJEC-
TIVES AND LAW EXAM
PROBLEM–QUESTIONS

a.   Objectives of Examinations in General—
Types of Questions

As a general proposition, and *not* with specific reference to law exams, the "examination" or "testing" procedures employed in
schools and other educational or training programs are attempts to determine and measure or evaluate, either objectively or judg-
mentally, one or more of the following things:

(1) Knowledge, comprehension and memory:
what one has *learned*, or *"knows"*, or
believes, or *understands*, *and remembers*
about particular matters;

(2) The *accuracy* of one's recall of knowledge and understanding, when that is determinable by some external referent or
standard;

(3) How effectively and accurately one can
communicate knowledge, beliefs, ideas

and other matters in language or other symbols;

(4) How skillfully and efficiently one can *use* and *apply* knowledge, beliefs and ideas in performing particular tasks or functions, mental or physical, in comparison with others;

(5) How rapidly (3) and (4) can be accomplished time-wise in an exam situation.

Examinations and other testing may also provide psychological motivation and reinforcement in learning, communicating and performing, and may serve other purposes, but these five seem to be the main objectives.

Various types of questions are used by examiners to obtain responses from examinees that will accurately indicate the extent of their attainments in these five respects. Determining (1) and (2)—the extent and accuracy of an examinee's recallable knowledge, belief or understanding of something, is not too difficult and is involved to some extent in all types of exam questions. If the examiner is testing only for accurate knowledge of simple facts the traditional, direct fact-questions are adequate: "Name the capitol cities of the 50 United States of America"; "What was the date of Beethoven's birth?"

"What are the elements of the tort of battery?" etc.

If more complex information or understanding of relationships or analogies must be tested, various types of "objective" exams may be most appropriate: e. g. true-false, multiple-choice or matching questions.

If determination of one's communication skills in reporting, narration, description or persuasion is the examiner's objective, an essay, theme or report may be used effectively as a test.

If determination of one's skills and abilities in the more complex mental processes of *using* and *applying* knowledge in analysis and logical reasoning is the objective, the use of problem-questions like those traditional in mathematics, physics or accounting exams is most effective.

b. Law Exams

Today few, if any, instructors or bar examiners use the type of exam made up of simple fact questions like "What is first-degree murder?" or "What is the rule in Shelley's Case?" or "What is the definition of an assault?". Such questions obviously test nothing but the extent and accuracy of the student's knowledge, and the answers merely show how many legal definitions, rules and exceptions he knows accurately and can recall. Such information can be obtained in questions that also test its significance and how well it can be used and applied.

In some law subjects, where there is a considerable body of technical information and non-controversial propositions or statutory or regulatory provisions which must be learned and understood in order to deal properly with the difficult problems, some law teachers use either an "objective" or "short-answer" exam to determine whether such material has been adequately mastered. Also, of course, in seminars or subjects like legal writing, trial practice, appellate advocacy, legislative drafting and the like, the testing of achievement is by the instructor's judgmental appraisal of required papers, memoranda, briefs, oral arguments, drafts of statutes, etc.

In the basic, first-year law courses, however, and in many later courses and most bar examinations, the tests consist largely or wholly of *problem-questions*—statements of fact-situations involving various types of legal problems or controversies and requiring some sort of decision as to how they probably would or should be resolved on the basis of applicable law. In principle and objective such questions are similar to the problems in a mathematics exam, but they are not as easy to answer properly because they require a skillful use of language in their solution rather than mathematical symbols and formulae.

Problem-questions are an excellent tool for testing many aspects of "lawyer ability" because they involve what lawyers constantly deal with—specific problems and controversies. Their value lies in the fact that they test most of the basic aptitudes, skills and knowledge that lawyers must have to do legal problem-solving with professional competence.

They require an understanding of legal *classifications* and the *organization* of the various fields of law because you first have to *classify* each problem, recognize what *general* type it is, and also what *specific* "*issues*" and legal questions are involved in it.

Problem questions also require an adequate *knowledge* and *understanding* of the cases, statutes, ordinances, administrative regulations, court rules, official interpretations, etc.

you've studied, and the *reasons* and policies underlying them. These are hereafter referred to collectively as "the law" to avoid lengthy repetition. Problems test your ability to recognize "the law" that may be applicable to each issue and distinguish that which is not. Even when there is no established "law" on a particular issue or question, or when "the law" on it is out-dated or seems unjust or inappropriate, problem-questions afford students an opportunity to use their imaginative and creative abilities and the ideas and theories encountered in their study of law review articles and legal treatises to formulate and suggest what they regard as appropriate, or more appropriate, rules for such issues and questions.

"The law", existing or suggested, is the basis (major premise) for your *reasoning* in deciding each issue in the problem and reaching conclusions and a decision on the question(s) asked. Thus, problem-questions require a demonstration of your ability to analyze creatively, argue logically, inductively and deductively, discriminate between situations that are superficially similar but that differ materially in one or more respects, and thus demonstrate your understanding of how the legal system operates in the decision of cases.

Finally, these problem-questions test your *language* and *writing* skills in organizing and presenting a clear, well-expressed opinion on the question(s) asked. You obviously do not have time in an exam to produce carefully worded, polished, legal writing. But lawyers often have to give informal written opinions and advice under considerable time-pressure and answering these problem-questions not only tests your ability to do this but helps you to develop it.

Learning how to answer this type of question properly is thus really a part of your legal education, and strange as it may seem, taking these exams can actually be an interesting and stimulating experience when you understand them, are adequately prepared and know what you are supposed to do.

c. What The Examiner Looks For In Answers To Problem Questions

Before going into the details of writing a proper answer, let's consider what things a law teacher or bar examiner is looking for and evaluating when he gives you these problems.

There is always a good deal of speculation in law school as to just what old Dean Glutz expects in an exam paper, or what you have to do to get a good grade from Prof. Soandso, or what you have to know in order to "pass the bar". In every school a venerable body of opinion on these matters is handed down from class to class, which some accept without ever bothering to ask the instructors about it. Even when some kind hearted teacher takes the trouble to explain what he expects, there are those who smile knowingly at his naive attempt to conceal the "real story" from *them*.

It is undoubtedly true that no two individual instructors or bar examiners are in full agreement as to what constitutes a perfect answer to a problem-question, or as to the relative importance of the various parts of it, and it would not only be foolish but impossible to tell you *exactly* what things each one wants emphasized in an answer without first asking him. Nevertheless, there are certain *fundamental* aspects of a good answer to a question of this type that all competent law teachers and examiners look for when they grade a paper, and those things can be explained.

First of all, remember that your answer is expected to be an *answer*. When you are given a set of facts and a question or questions about them, you are expected to *answer the questions asked*. Don't assume that these problems are prepared merely to give you an opportunity to regurgitate all the rules and cases you can remember. When a client goes to a lawyer with his problems, he wants a solution of those problems and not general legal information. When a case comes before a court for decision the judge wants arguments and memoranda dealing with the issues in *that* case. When an examiner gives you a problem question, he is looking for your answer(s) to his question(s) about *that* problem. He wants to find out whether you have the ability to do what all lawyers are expected to be able to do, namely, properly apply their legal knowledge and skills in solving their client's problem. The main object of law study is to develop all aspects of that ability, and he wants to discover whether you are achieving that object.

A mere "yes" or "no" or simple conclusion, however, is not a sufficient answer. Even judges give *reasons* for their decisions, and you are supposed to do the same. The examiner expects you to support your conclusions with arguments based upon the relevant "law" you have studied.   Thus, your answer should be a concise legal *opinion* similar to those handed down by courts.   You are expected to explain *why* you think "the law" requires the particular decision you are making.   So don't write your answer from the standpoint of a student telling his instructor what he has learned about law.   *Pretend that you are a lawyer* and that the problem-question is one that has been submitted to you by your client, or for him by a senior partner in your law firm, or by your employer.   Write your answer *as a lawyer would* in giving his analysis, reasoning and opinion or conclusion. This enables the examiner to appraise how well you can do such lawyer-tasks.

Assuming that you comply with these general requirements and give the examiner a definite answer to the question he asks with a clear, concise argument in support of it, what specific things does he look for in that argument?   What are the important parts—the things on which your grade depends?

In the first place he considers how many of the *issues* involved in the problem you have discussed.   Almost every legal problem and controversy involves a number of subsidiary issues, specific questions of law or fact, that must be decided before a final conclusion can be reached. When a lawyer gets a case he first must ascertain all the available, provable facts that have any bearing on the legality of what occurred. His next task, like that of a doctor, is *diagnosis.* He has to consider all of the possible legal rights, interests, causes of action, bases of civil or criminal liability or other legal wrongs that may be involved, as well as the possible privileges and defenses that may be asserted. He can't go to the books to find out what statutes, regulations, decisions or other "law" may govern his case, any more than a doctor can look up a proper treatment, until he has determined what type of case he has and what law to look for. If he overlooks a possible issue, his conclusion and argument may be seriously weakened.

In an exam problem you are *given* the facts. The value and soundness of your argument and conclusion depend upon whether, in light of all of "the law" and legal theory you have studied, you have accurately classified the specific problem given you and considered all of the possible legal issues on which the decision might depend in view of the facts given. To the extent that you have failed to recognize issues relevant to the facts of the problem your grade suffers. Many students have difficulty in determining which legal issues are *relevant* to a problem and should be mentioned and discussed in the answer and which are *irrelevant* and should not be discussed. The *facts* given in the problem or inferrable from those expressly stated and *the question* asked about them are the key to the relevant legal issues. A specific legal question that must be *decided*, if raised, in order to answer the problem-question on the facts given is relevant. A legal question and rule applicable only to a wholly different situation from the one in the problem is not relevant. If you have doubts about the relevance of a legal issue ask yourself: Are there *any facts* in this case to which that issue applies? If so, it is relevant and should be raised and answered even though the answer is obvious. If not, it is irrelevant to the decision of this case and should not be discussed.

The next thing the examiner looks for is your statement or explanation of "the law" or suggested law on which you are basing your argument and decision. Granting that you have recognized the relevant issues, he

[*113*]

wants to know whether you understand "the law" applicable to such issues. After all, if you're going to decide the issues according to law (as you are expected to do) you have to have a fairly accurate understanding of *what* *"the law" is* on each issue if there is any, whether it is well settled or uncertain, and the *reasons* on which it is based. If it happens that your problem involves an issue that is not governed by any established "law" he wants to see whether you know that fact and what rule you think a court might adopt in view of analogous cases and relevant principles, policies and theories.

Lastly, the examiner looks for your *reasoning*—your *application* of the pertinent law to the facts he has given you. No two legal controversies are exactly alike in every detail, and although the problem you are deciding may be quite similar to others you have studied, there may be some aspect of it that requires a different decision. He wants to see whether you recognize the similarities and differences in facts and whether, by reference to the *reasons* and *policies* underlying "the law" involved, you have arrived at a logical and sound conclusion as to these facts.

Issues—"The Law" or Suggested Law on Each Issue—Its Application to These Facts—Conclusions and Decision.

Those are the basic elements of a good legal argument and those are the things the examiner is looking for in your answer. As previously indicated, it's impossible to tell you just how much value your particular instructor or bar examiner attaches to each of these elements, or the ones he thinks are the most important. You'll have to find that out from him. In that connection, however, there are one or two things to bear in mind.

In the first place, each instructor in law school is testing you on the basis of a definite body of "law" that has been covered in his course. He knows what's been covered and what hasn't. Ordinarily he does not give you problems involving phases of law that are wholly unfamiliar or that have not been referred to in the course. Consequently, he usually expects you to know and understand the pertinent law quite thoroughly, including the unclear statutes, the conflicting decisions and views, the reasons for these and so on. Furthermore, he normally expects you to confine your discussion to the legal questions pertinent to his course, and not discuss those

dealt with in other courses even though the
problem may involve them.

Bar examiners, on the other hand, are dealing with students from many different law
schools whose courses in various subjects normally differ in content. Consequently, bar
examiners do not know exactly what material
each of you has studied in each subject and,
in selecting problem-questions, they are to
some extent "shooting in the dark". Most of
them realize that some of their problems will
be utterly strange to some of you and that
your answers and discussions will have to be
based on the broad general principles and
policies you have learned rather than on specific cases or statutes. Generally, bar examiners do not expect or require as thorough
and accurate an understanding of detailed
law as a law teacher does. Nevertheless, bar
examiners differ greatly from state to state
and it is difficult to generalize about what
they want. Many of them do expect a fairly
detailed understanding of the principal statutes, decisions and court rules in their own
state, but on the whole their grades are based
more on your analysis of the problem and
your ability to present a sound, logical argument in support of your conclusions than on

the number of statutes, cases or court rules you can accurately remember.

Another thing to keep in mind is that bar exam problems are selected from a large number of subjects and tend to be less complex than law school problems. In many of them the problems are not labeled with such titles as Torts, Property, Procedure, etc., and a single problem may contain issues involving material you have dealt with in several different courses. Even in those exams where the problems are labeled under conventional headings, they may not be of the same type as those you considered in the law school courses so labeled. Thus a bar exam problem listed under the heading of "Contracts" may involve questions of Specific Performance which you may have studied in a course in Remedies. Or a problem classified under "Evidence" may deal wholly with the Parol Evidence Rule which you perhaps studied in your course in Contracts. Nevertheless, you will be expected to discuss all relevant issues in these problems and will therefore have to analyze them on a much broader legal basis than you did the problems in your school exams.

In view of these and other differences between law school and bar exams, it is wise to get as much *reliable* information as you can about the type of bar exam given in your state and what the examiners require. Don't rely on mere rumor, however. Ask someone who knows. In many states it is helpful, and sometimes almost essential, to enroll in a bar review or cram course. These differ greatly in price, quality and usefulness, so inquire about them from some responsible young lawyer before signing up.

d.   Writing the Answers

If you keep in mind the preceding explanation of the nature and object of problem-questions and the things the examiner looks for in your answer you shouldn't have much trouble in writing good answers, provided, of course, you have the necessary native ability for legal work and have done a proper and thorough job of studying. Nevertheless, some specific suggestions about the actual procedure of writing answers may be helpful. Most of us are inclined to "clutch" a little and get the jitters when we actually find ourselves in the exam room, and it helps a lot to have some definite, specific ideas about what to do and what not to do.

Some examiners recommend that you first real *all* the problems in an exam before try-

read   [*118*]

ing to answer any of them, to get a better perspective and see which problems deal with which parts of the course. This is helpful, but you may find it confusing, especially if you are nervous or apprehensive, and you may prefer to deal with them one at a time and answer each before you even look at the next. Whichever approach you adopt, be sure to *apportion your time* in view of the number of problems and questions and try to stay on schedule. Don't spend so much time on the first questions that you have to hurry through the others. Also, don't discuss matters that are *not relevant* to the facts of the problem and the question asked. Above all, don't panic and start writing before you know what you want to say. You'll usually be given adequate time to finish the whole exam and do a good job if you don't waste it on irrelevant discussion. The secret of writing a good paper without wasting time is to work *systematically*.

Spend at least a third of the allotted time *reading* the problem, *thinking* about the question asked, *analyzing* the problem and *planning* your answer before you write anything. You can't build a good house unless you've first determined what kind of a house you want and have some plans. You can't write a good answer until you've thoroughly read the problem, analyzed it thoroughly in light of the relevant law and determined what issues need discussion in order to answer the question(s) asked. This, of course, seems obvious, but the urge to start writing is frequently so strong you may forget it unless you follow a definite program. It's impossible, of course, to tell you exactly how to proceed Problems vary and human minds work differently. There are, however, several basic steps that have to be taken, and the following suggestions may prove helpful to you in working out your own systematic program.

1.   Reading the Problem

First get the facts straight. Understand who the parties are, what they did, and what happened to them. Pay particular attention to the *question(s) asked*, and exactly what you are told to decide—whose rights or what liabilities are involved. Read the whole problem through at least *twice*. The first time you read one of these problem questions it nearly always seems strange and unfamiliar. Read it again, slowly and thoroughly, line by line and phrase by phrase. You'll find a lot of things you missed the first time. Try to visualize the situation that's described. Draw a diagram on scratch paper if the facts are complicated. It doesn't take long to do this, and when you really understand the fact situation you'll usually find that the problem is not so unfamiliar as it seemed at first. Above all, be sure you haven't *misread* what is stated or *misunderstood* the question. That's inexcusable and will spoil your whole answer. Furthermore, *don't assume facts that are neither stated nor inferable from those that are*, unless of course the question *asks* whether additional facts are needed for a decision.

2. *Analysis*

In analyzing a problem start with the question(s) asked or the statement of what you are to decide. That's the focal point of the whole problem. Then figure out, step by step, what the answer depends upon in view of the facts given and the law you have studied. In other words, determine all the subordinate questions and the ultimate, specific issues of law and fact that will have to be decided before you can make your decision on the main question. Then determine how those ultimate issues ought to be decided in view of "the law" applicable to them. Perhaps the best way to explain this process is to illustrate it. Suppose that you were given the following simple problem in a Contracts exam:

"B owed A $1000 presently due. A wrote a letter to B on May 1st, telling him that he, A, needed money and that if B would send him a money order for $750 A would cancel the $1000 debt. B received this letter on May 3rd, but did nothing until May 11th. On that day B wrote A, enclosing a bank money order, payable to A, for $750 and requesting a receipt in full for the debt. A received this letter on May 13th, but immediately wired B that he would not accept the $750 as full payment, that B had waited too long and that A now demanded the $250 balance of the debt. B refused to pay any more. Has A a cause of action against B for the $250?

(The question might, of course, be stated in various ways. For example:

"Is A entitled to recover anything from B?"

"A brought an action against B for $250. Decide the case."

"A brought an action against B for $250, alleging the foregoing facts in his complaint. B moved to dismiss the complaint. Should the motion be granted?

In any of these forms, however, the question still calls for a determination of A's rights against B, with respect to the balance of the $1000 debt.)

In analyzing this problem you would observe that the answer obviously depends upon whether A's promise to cancel the debt became legally binding on him when he received the $750. If it did, he clearly has no rights against B. If it did not, however, the debt has not yet been fully paid and A has a cause of action against B for the balance. Whether the promise was legally binding on A depends, of course, upon the law governing the legal enforceability of promises in general, and you would therefore go back mentally over the various cases and statutes you have studied which dealt with that question, and determine whether all the requirements are present in this situation. You would recall the general rule that simple, unsealed promises (like A's) are not ordinarily legally binding unless they are part of an agreement and supported by legally sufficient consideration. Thus, unless there was an *agreement* reached between A and B—an offer and acceptance—and legally sufficient consideration, A's promise was not binding on him. Mentally reviewing "the law" dealing with offers, you will probably conclude that A's promise in his letter was clearly an offer to B requesting an *act* on B's part (offer for unilateral contract), and that since it specified no time for acceptance it remained open for a reasonable time. Since B clearly did the requested act and thus purported to accept the offer unconditionally, the only debatable point on the question of offer and acceptance is whether he did the act within a reasonable time, and that would be the first ultimate issue. But even if B did accept A's offer within a reasonable time and thus consummated an *agreement* with him, A still would not be bound unless his promise was supported by a legally sufficient consideration. Mentally going over "the law" on that subject you would recall the conflict in the cases and statutes as to whether a debtor's payment of part of a presently due, liquidated debt in return for the creditor's promise to cancel the whole debt is sufficient consideration, on policy grounds, to bind the creditor. That would be another ultimate issue. Then, to be sure that the facts involved no other legal questions on which A's rights might depend, you would mentally go over the other general rules governing the legal enforceability of promises to see whether any of them might be applicable. Finding none, you would then reason out your conclusions on the two issues found. On the issue of reasonable time you might conclude that the question was simply one of fact, that it was sufficiently doubtful to go to a jury, and that it could properly be decided either way. On the issue of consideration you would recall that despite persuasive reasons and a few decisions and statutes to the contrary most of the cases have held that part payment was not sufficient consideration in a situation like this and, although the point could be plausibly argued either way, you might well conclude that A's promise in this case would not be legally binding on him, and that he is therefore entitled to recover the balance of the $1000 debt from B.

This description of the reasoning you would presumably follow in analyzing the suggested problem is, of course, merely illustrative. It is simply an attempt to indicate the sort of mental process you have to go through, consciously or subconsciously, in determining the answer to any legal problem. It is not set forth as an ideal pattern that should always be followed even in analyzing this specific problem.

In many instances you will immediately recognize some of the ultimate issues involved in a problem as soon as you have read it. In others you will have to go through a complex series of logical propositions and consider numerous possibilities before you discover the basic issues involved. The important thing is to understand what you are trying to do and then do it thoroughly. Be sure you have found and considered *all* the *arguable* questions that might be involved on the facts given and "the law" you have studied. Don't be content to give a decision based solely on your conclusion as to one issue when a contrary conclusion on that issue would require a consideration of further questions. Exhaust all the possibilities. On the other hand, when you have found all the issues that *seem* pertinent, consider them carefully to see whether they really are involved on the facts of the problem, or whether, in view of the facts, they could not properly be raised. Don't try to reach or support a decision by an argument that is not applicable to the facts.

3.   *Planning the Answer*

Before you start writing, take a moment or two to plan the best order in which to discuss the issues. Don't just start writing and then try to organize what you've written by re-writing, crossing out, interlineating and inserting arrows. Work out a logical sequence in which to discuss the various issues and then follow it. Writing takes far more time than thinking. One or two minutes spent in organizing may save ten minutes wasted in writing a page that has to be crossed out. Furthermore, remember that you're building a structure of ideas for someone else to examine and that it will be better understood if the basic propositions that form the foundation appear before the superstructure that rests upon them.

4. *Writing*

When you come to the actual process of stating your decision and argument, remember first of all that the *examiner is not a mind reader*. He hasn't been with you in spirit while you analyzed the problem and he doesn't know how much or how little you know. Further, you can not expect him to *presume*, without your proof, that you've seen the issues, understood the relevant law and its application to the facts and drawn appropriate conclusions. On such presumptions a "yes" or "no" on a blank page would be a perfect answer. The presumption is that you *don't* know and can't do these things. You have to rebut that presumption by an affirmative showing that you can. Consequently in discussing each issue you should first indicate briefly *what it is* and *why* it has to be considered. Mention the statutes, regulations or cases that make it pertinent and state which ones you think are controlling in view of the reasons for them and the facts given. If "the law" is in conflict, or if the facts in this problem seem materially different from those in other similar cases, discuss those conflicts and the fact distinctions, and indicate *why* you think your conclusion ought to be drawn rather than another. In short, tell the examiner what each issue is, what "the law" is, the reasons for it, and *why* you think it is applicable and should be applied on these facts. Don't simply state a conclusion and expect him to guess what reasons you had in your mind for reaching it.

Another thing to remember is to make your answer *readable* and *coherent*. The only thing the examiner has to go on is the writing on your paper. He's not ordinarily an expert in deciphering secret codes or short-hand, so make your writing both legible and intelligible. Observe what you've learned about grammar, punctuation and spelling. When you can't even spell a term properly, it's difficult to convince a reader that you know what it means. Remember that in writing an answer you're trying to show the examiner that you understand the problem and *convince* him that your solution is right. It's your job to make your ideas clear to him, not his job to figure out what you're trying to say.

SECTION 2. ILLUSTRATIVE PROBLEM QUESTIONS WITH SAMPLE ANSWERS AND COMMENTS

There are many forms of problem-questions, some simple and fairly easy, some complex and difficult, some long, some short, some with few issues and some involving many. There are also a variety of forms and styles in which a good answer to a problem-question may be written. There is no one "right" way to the exclusion of all others, although, as explained above, there are certain *essential matters* that must be presented, in one way or another, in any satisfactory answer.

The following problems, each followed by a sample of a Good "A" Answer and a Mar-

[*129*]

ginal Answer, have been assembled as illustrations for use in reviewing and preparing for first-year law exams. Where helpful,
a Comment on a problem or an answer has
been added.

The method of using these problems and
answers in reviewing and preparing for exams is explained in Part I of the book, Section 9, pages 96–98.

CONTRACTS REMEDIES

(one hour)

Super Pancake Co. owns recipes and flour-mix formulas for a variety of delicious pancakes. It also owns several sets of specially designed building, equipment and lay-out plans for pancake-house eating establishments plus well-developed systems for operating all phases of such establishments plus contract arrangements with suppliers of the various materials and equipment needed to build, equip and operate them. S Co. does not itself own and operate such establishments but makes franchise contracts with people in many midwest cities who build and operate them in accordance with S Co's plans and under detailed licensing, supply and credit arrangements spelled out in the contracts. In May, 1970, B, who for 10 years had been successfully managing a small, hamburger drive-in, desired to make one of these contracts with S Co. and build, own and operate a "Super Pancake House" in a Minneapolis suburb. B found a suitable lot which O, its owner, offered to sell to B for $15,000. B bought from O a six-months option on the lot at that price, paying O $500 for the op-

tion. B received from his bank assurances
of financing for the building, opened negotiations with S Co. and, after 3 months of
proposals and counter-proposals, B and S Co.
signed, in August, 1970, one of S Co's franchise contracts giving B the exclusive right
to operate a "Super Pancake House" on the
O lot for 10 years beginning March 1, 1971,
but with a provision giving either B or S Co.
the power to terminate at the end of February, 1973, or on any subsequent March 1st,
if B's gross business receipts for the previous
year fell below a figure specified in the contract. B thereupon bought the lot from O,
paying him $15,000; obtained a financing
commitment from the bank for the building;
and made a contract with a contractor, C, to
erect it in accordance with S Co's plan. B
had intended to continue on his job as manager of the drive-in (salary: $750 per month)
until March 1st, 1971, when the pancake
house was scheduled for completion, but when
the owner of the drive-in learned of B's plans,
in September, 1970, he hired a new manager
and discharged B. On September 30th, just
as C was beginning construction, B received
a letter from the president of S Co. stating
that because of depressed business conditions
and tight credit the Co's directors had de-

termined not to proceed with any new outlets and that S Co. was therefore canceling its contract with B. Assume that this would be held to be a breach of contract by S Co.

(1) If, on October 1st, B had consulted his lawyer and asked (a) whether he, B, could legally compel S Co. to proceed with the contract and (b) whether he should order contractor C to stop further construction, what should the lawyer have advised him? State in a concise opinion your conclusions on each question with the legal reasons therefor.

(2) Assume that B decided *not* to try to force S Co. to proceed; that B has had to pay C $2,000 to reimburse him for his expenditures and to obtain from C a release from the construction contract; that B listed the lot for sale, has not found a buyer, must now pay $400 in 1971 real estate taxes on it, and has been advised by three real estate experts that in the present market he probably cannot get more than $12,000 net for it; that he has figures, furnished by S Co. during negotiations, showing the 1969 net profits of 3 of its pancake houses in other cities. These are $20,000, $34,000 and $50,000. B has also obtained 1970 net profit figures from two Perkins Pancake houses in the Twin City area. These are $25,000 and $42,000. So

far B has been unsuccessful in finding a job
and is borrowing money to live on. If B sues
S Co. for damages for breach of contract
what amounts would he probably be legally
entitled to recover under various rules of
damages law and what would probably be his
best basis for claiming damages?

.   .   .   .   .

**COMMENT: This problem involves many is-
sues and sub-issues under the rules governing
remedies for breach of contract. In answering it, there would not be time for extended
discussion of each issue and the answer on
each would thus necessarily have to be short
and concise. Grading the answers would
therefore have to be based largely upon how
many of the possible issues each answer dealt
with rather than upon the depth of analysis
of particular issues. As a basis for grading,
the instructor might, therefore, prepare and
use simply an "issue summary" like the following:**

PROFESSOR'S SUMMARY OF RELEVANT
    ISSUES AND SUB-ISSUES FOR USE
    AS A CHECK-LIST IN GRADING THE
    ANSWERS

——Would Statutes of Frauds bar B's
    claims? K not performable "within 1

year"?   Does detailed signed writing comply with S/F requirements?

(1) (a) Can B obtain specific performance by S Co.?

Adequacy of damages-remedy:

——Was this K *unique*—could B readily obtain a similar franchise?

——Would damages for value of S Co.'s performance be difficult to measure?

Feasibility of Spec. perf:

——Is the continuing relationship under this K too complex for decree?

——Too "personal" or confidential and judgmental?

——Other factors?   Hardship on S Co? Third parties?

——Advice to B on compelling S Co. to continue?

(1) (b) Should B order contractor C to stop construction?

——Mitigation   requirement—Rockingham Co. bridge case: "Pile-up" damages?

——Does it apply if B seeks specific performance?

——Does mitigation require B to incur liability to C for breach of the construction K by ordering stoppage?

——Was this an anticipatory breach allowing B to wait a reasonable time?

——Advice to B on ordering C to stop?

(2) Action vs. S Co. for damages—possible amounts recoverable?

——Can objective of putting B in as good a position as performance be achieved? Does loss of S Co's promised performance amount to B's *lost net profits*?

——Can am't of B's lost profits per year be determined with sufficient definiteness to avoid rule against "speculation and conjecture"?

——Uncertainties of new business; new location; B's experience, etc.

——What period of time; 2 years? 10 years?

——*Consequential damage from breach:* $2,000 to settle with C?

——Were these foreseeable under Hadley v. Baxendale?

——*Reliance losses* per Dempsey and Security Stove cases?

——As alternative to lost profits?   Not both?

——No recovery for the $500 cost of option —incurred before K? not in reliance? B assumed the risk as to this—Dempsey case (Wills K)?

But how about:

——$3000 loss on purchase of lot? ($15,000 —$12,000) Was this foreseeable? Too indefinite?

——Was this foreseeable as a risk of the K?

——$400 *real estate taxes*? Avoidable? Foreseeable?

——$3750 (5 x $750) *loss of salary*, Oct. thru Feb.? Was this in *reliance* on K?

——S Co. have burden of proving B could have found similar work?

——Was this a *foreseeable* consequence of making the K? Hadley case?

——Was the money borrowed to live on an alternative to salary and the same value?

——Costs of financing commitment, if any? Other expenditures?

——Restitution? Any evidence of enrichment/benefit by S Co?

.   .   .   .   .   .

[*137*]

COMMENT: Using the foregoing summary as a standard, the following two answers illustrate the difference between what would be considered a good "A" answer and a marginal (low C or D) answer:

ANSWERS TO CONTRACTS REMEDIES PROBLEM

GOOD "A" ANSWER

(K means contract)

I(a) We first note that the K which B might seek to have enforced, is written, thereby complying with the Statute of Frauds, (assuming, as we probably can because of the details included in franchise K's, that all of the essential elements of a memo of the transaction are included) should the K be within the Statute, on the theory that it is not capable of being performed within one year, by its very terms.

Possibility of Specific Performance— Although specific performance is presumed to be appropriate in contracts for the sale of land, it is also available with other K's, should the K's and the circumstances meet the required tests.

[*133*]

The franchise K here would not seem to meet the requirements necessary before specific performance is usually granted. First, although S breached because of economic conditions, S might be able to claim that the court should not compel S to enter into such a relationship with B against S's will. Nevertheless S is a corporation, so this argument is not as compelling as in a continuing personal service K involving two individuals.

Secondly, the *requirement of feasibility*. Although the court could clearly compel S to comply with the K, and the terms of the K are apparently spelled out in detail, the peculiar nature of the franchise K which necessitates a close and cooperative and continuing relationship between the parties, makes it unlikely that the court would order specific performance. I doubt that the court would favor specific performance in K's involving long, continuing and complex relationships which could easily lead to litigation in the future.

Thirdly, *adequacy of legal damages*. B could make a stronger case here that legal damages would be inadequate. The value of the promised performance of the franchise includes, as its main part, the profits B would hope to make from the operation. Although B has successfully managed a *similar* operation, and he has figures on the profitability of similar establishments, I doubt that these would satisfy because of the *Rule against Speculation and Conjecture*.

His alternative damages are unlikely, similarly, to adequately compensate him: The $500 for the option K was incurred before the franchise; the lost wages resulting from early termination of his previous job arguably were not consequential and were insufficiently foreseeable. No evidence, though there might be, that franchise is unique. B might be able to get another one elsewhere.

But in view of the presumption against specific performance (except in land K's) a court probably would not order specific performance.

I(b) B should definitely order C to stop construction. A party is not permitted to pile up damages when the other party repudiates. Here, S appeared to repudiate absolutely. The building, which was being built according to S's special plans for its own operation, is probably so unique that it might be wasteful to continue construction if it cannot be put to intended use. Thus with S's anticipatory repudiation, B should be ordered to cease construction. It's likely that any K liability B has to C can be collected from S as reliance damages.

II. *Value of promised performance.* The general goal is to put B where he would have been if S had performed fully. In a franchise K, the value of the promised performance is probably best measured (as B would measure it) by the net profits to be realized from operations.

Yet the evidence B has on this measure (since B has no record of operations, because S's breach was anticipatory) would probably fall under the Rule against Speculation and Conjecture, both as to the Perkins figures, and the S figures from other cities, especially in view of B's lack of experience in managing a Pancake restaurant, as opposed to the small hamburger drive-in.

B could certainly collect *nominal* damages since S's breach is clear, and the damages aren't, but this is unsatisfactory because it fails to adequately compensate B.

B might be able to collect on alternative theories to value of promised performance. Particularly, the *reliance* theory. (Restitution is probably not applicable because it is used to prevent unjust enrichment. Here, B's partial performance probably has conferred no benefit on S, so nothing to award to B on that basis.)

Reliance damages

The $500 for the option K was incurred *before* the franchise K, so probably not recoverable, as B cannot be said to have reasonably relied on S's expected performance before S entered the K.

The land purchase by B was clearly in reliance on S's expected performance, and it's clear that if B sells now he will lose $3000. It's doubtful whether S should be liable for the apparent bad

[*142*]

bargain B made, although if the land has been reduced in value by C's operations on it, B can probably collect.

The $2000 payment to C—B entered the K with C clearly and reasonably in reliance on S's expected performance. B can probably collect, since the costs are of no value to B after S's repudiation. Same arguments might apply to *real estate taxes*.

Loss of income. Might be claimed under "consequential" damages theory, but I doubt that they were foreseeable to S, at the time of the K, sufficiently to satisfy the rule in the Hadley case, since apparently even B was not expecting to be terminated.

Same argument applies to the living expenses B is now borrowing for. It's clear that he would have had them even if S had performed, and S could not be expected to foresee them as a consequence of the breach. Here B is under a clear duty to mitigate if reasonably possible. S certainly is not liable for the period up to the time B's operations should have commenced.

.   .   .   .   .   .

COMMENT: This is not a perfect answer. Few are. But this discusses adequately about 80% of the total, relevant issues involved including all of the major ones. It is well-organized, concise, clear and articulate; indicates the applicable rules on most issues, and analyzes briefly the relevant facts bearing on each.

MARGINAL ANSWER

I.   I would opt for specific performance but I would also advise B that his chances for getting specific performance—compelling S Co. to proceed with the contract—were slim, but not impossible. Unlike the Grayson-Robinson case, here there was no arbitration decision to order specific performance, and no "easement" clause in the contract between B and S Co. The court would be reluctant to force S Co. into any sort of servitude. However, since the terms of the contract appear only to involve the S. Co.'s providing plans, "secret recipes" and their name, the granting of specific performance might be allowed. If B were to allow C to continue construction and the court ruled that S Co. had successfully repudiated the contract, then B would be stuck with the expense of construction incurred after the date of repudiation. The duty to mitigate damages would fall on B.

The potential gain by B's receiving specific enforcement would be larger than his potential recovery for breach and damages (as explained next).

II. I think it is clear that if B were to sue S Co. for breach of contract, B could recover:

A) The $2,000 expenditure to C for work done before the breach. This is money that B is out for his *reliance* on the contract.

B) $3,000 for the difference in land values. B entered hastily into a "bad" bargain in reliance on the contract with S Co.

I don't think B would be able to recover:

A) The $400 in real estate taxes. This is money B would have been out whether the contract was breached or not.

B) Any amount stemming from the *expectation* interest of B in future profits. With the admittedly unstable situation in the economy these profit figures for other establishments are no clear indication that B would make a profit at any time in the future or in what amount if any.

[*145*]

C) The salary foregone. B was fired and if
S Co. had fulfilled their contract they certainly would not be liable for B's loss of
wages. There is some sentiment to allow
B to recover his lost wages as a form of
"restitution interest"—(to put B back to the
economic position he was in to start), but S
Co. was not directly responsible for B's firing
and it would be unjust to hold S Co. liable
for the acts of a third party.

I think B's best basis for recovering damages would be the theory of his money spent
in reliance of S Co.'s K. He may be able
to work something up along the lines of the
value of his K. If the court would buy the
average profit figures of the identical franchises in other cities and similar franchises
in the Twin Cities, and further conclude
that B's chances for making a similar profit
would have been good if the K had been fulfilled, then they might have allowed him to
recover this profit foregone for the 2 years
potential the K had.

.   .   .   .   .   .

**COMMENT: This is not a hopelessly inade-
quate or failing answer; it would receive a
D or low-C grade by most instructors. It
answers the questions asked and is organ-**

ized, but consists mainly of a series of conclusions with very little in the way of supporting reasons for them or reference to the cases or rules of law involved. Furthermore, there is some error and confusion as to restitution and reliance interests. This answer deals only with the most obvious issues involved and fails to mention many of the subissues, ramifications and alternatives dealt with in the "A" answer. Over-all it deals only with about one-third of the points that could properly be discussed as relevant to the possible decisions on the questions asked.

CONTRACTS (I)

(one hour)

X was knocked down and rendered unconscious by a bus operated by B Bus Co. The bus driver, in accordance with the Company's general instructions, called an ambulance, had X taken to the nearest hospital and promptly reported the accident to company officials. X was x-rayed and given emergency treatment by the physician on emergency duty at the hospital and regained consciousness within two hours. An hour or two thereafter a claim agent of B Co. called at X's bedside, identified himself, asked a few questions which X seemed to answer coherently, and then asked to see the physician who had attended X. When the physician came to X's room the agent asked about X's injuries. The physician told both X and the agent that the x-rays showed no fractures and that X had no internal bleeding; that in his opinion X was suffering from slight shock and superficial cuts and bruises; and that X could leave the hospital the next day and should be able to return to work in two or three days. The agent told X he was lucky since the Bus Co. did not admit liability for the accident. He told X that "to avoid disputes and hard feelings" the Co. would "take care of the hospital bill and pay you $200 for your inconvenience" if X would sign a "release". The agent then filled out a short, partly printed form, headed "Release and Settlement Agreement" which stated that "In consideration of $200 paid" by B Bus Co. to X he "hereby releases the company from all liability and relinquishes all claims against it for injuries and damage of every kind, known or unknown, caused by the accident" . . . (Agent here filled in accurately the time and location of the accident) . . . "This contains the whole agreement; any representations or statements not contained herein are not authorized or binding on the company." The agent handed this to X, saying, "If you want the $200, sign this and send it to the company and they'll send you a check. If anything else develops we'll take care of it. We want to be fair." X was discharged from the hospital the next morning and two days later returned to his job as bookkeeper. The day he started work he signed and mailed the form to the company, and two days later received its check for $200 which he cashed. Two days after that, X collapsed at his work and was taken to the hospital where it was determined that he had suffered a concussion of the brain, which will incapacitate him for at least six months. The Bus Co. denies all liability for this and also refuses to pay X's first hospital bill.

(1) If the Release Agreement is valid and binding can X recover the amount of his first hospital bill from B Bus Co.? Reasons?

(2) Assume that X has a good negligence case for all damages and expense from the accident unless such action is barred by the Release Agreement. Is it? Indicate the possibilities and chances of avoiding it and the steps that you as X's lawyer would advise him to take.

.   .   .   .   .   .

ANSWERS TO CONTRACTS (I)
CONSISTENCY

GOOD "A" ANSWER

(1) Assuming that the Release Agreement is valid and binding X probably can*not* recover the amount of his first hospital bill. The signed Agreement was fully in writing, did not mention the hospital bill and contained an "integration clause" specifying that it contained "the whole agreement" and that representations or statements not con-

[*150*]

tained in it "were not authorized or binding on the company". By such provision and also under the Parol Evidence Rule no prior or contemporaneous oral agreement between X and Agent that would add to or contradict the writing could be asserted by either party. An attempt by X to show that before he signed Agent had promised that the Company "would take care of the hospital bill *and* pay" $200 would be an attempt to *add* an obligation not assumed by the Company in the writing and would not be permitted.

(2) Whether the Agreement bars X's negligence action depends upon its legal validity. It was a settlement agreement by which X bargained to give up and release his unliquidated claim for damages against the Bus Co. in return for $200, which the Co. paid. There were both mutual assent and consideration since the Co. did not admit liability but nevertheless paid $200, and X gave up his right to recover more. The essentials of a contract were present.

However, if there was incapacity or mutual mistake, or if the Agent did not act in good faith, took unconscionable advantage of X or was guilty of deceit or misrepresentation, a court would hold the agreement

[*151*]

voidable. But X cannot keep the $200 and also avoid the Release so I would advise him to return the money to the Company, claim that the Release was void and sue in tort. To avoid the Company's defense of the Release, several possibilities exist.

The first step might be to claim incapacity. If at the time X signed the release, he was actually in such a state of shock that he did not know what he was doing, the agreement would be voidable. It is unlikely, however, that such incapacity could be shown since X returned to the job right after signing and did not collapse until later.

A second possible claim is that the contract was obtained through the doctor's misrepresentation as to X's condition, without which the agreement wouldn't have been signed. However, it does not appear that the doctor worked for the Company so such a result is doubtful. Moreover, if the concussion wasn't discoverable at the time, there wouldn't even be a misrepresentation of existing fact, which is necessary.

Third, it could be claimed that because of a mutual mistake as to the identity or existence of the subject matter of the agreement it is voidable. This claim, like the other two, can be based upon extrinsic evidence because the parol evidence rule doesn't apply in determining the validity of the contract. In this case, both parties were acting under the assumption that there was no major injury to X, and he surely did not actually intend to assume for $200 the risk that there might be such injury. But the form contained the express statement "damages known or unknown". Unless X can prove that he did not read the Release, which he normally is charged with doing when he signed it, or was misled by Agent and did not understand this provision because of Agent's statement about taking care of "anything else" that developed, he would not succeed on this claim of mutual mistake because he would be deemed to have assumed the risk of unknown injury. It would be worth arguing this claim, however,

Fourth, it might be argued that Agent's oral promise to pay for "anything else" that developed was made subsequent to the written agreement, and that this was a modification of the contract. This is permitted under Graziano. Written contracts can be modified by subsequent oral agreements and evidence can be admitted to show such modifications. However, this agreement

[*153*]

was actually signed after X returned home and therefore it is hard to say that the Agent's oral promise at the hospital subsequently modified the written release, unless the court would hold that the agreement was made at the hospital and not when X signed and sent the release. Even then the oral and written agreements were probably made contemporaneously, so the oral agreement can't be admitted on these grounds.

Fifth, if it is possible to show by clear and convincing evidence that the actual intent of both X and Agent was to compensate X for future injuries and that both parties orally agreed to this, reformation might possibly be allowed, and the extrinsic evidence admitted for this purpose. Yet, this is usually permitted only when there was a mutual mistake in drawing up the writing, and the facts do not seem to indicate such a mistake. The necessary evidence is probably not clear and convincing enough in this case for reformation.

Sixth, it could be argued persuasively that the contract in question was so unconscionable as to justify its avoidance. In effect, the Bus Co. is contracting out of its possibly extensive liability for negligence for a mere $200. As the dissent in O'Callaghan stated, this type of agreement could be against public policy and not be permitted, at least in cases like this where the Agent was not really acting in good faith because he promised orally to pay X for future damage when the writing stated otherwise.

Seventh, it could be plausibly argued that the contract should also be avoided on grounds of deceit in what the Agent represented to X. He said that the Co. would compensate for "anything else" and X relied on this in signing the agreement. Since the Agent must have known of the "known or unknown damages" provision he knew his promise was false and never intended to compensate X. This would be a misrepresentation as to an existing fact, Agent's intention, which would justify recission. Either of these last two arguments could be successful if X could be shown to have reasonably relied on the promise which he seems to have done. This wouldn't violate the parol evidence rule because it shows that the contract wasn't valid.

.   .   .   .   .   .

COMMENT: This answer deals with most of the possible issues in this fairly difficult problem of contract avoidability. The various

bases for attacking the Release and the ob-
stacles posed by the Parol Evidence Rule and
integration clause are reasonably well argued
and presented, and the applicable rules and
cases are indicated at least by implication.

.   .   .   .   .   .

MARGINAL ANSWER

(1) If the release agreement is valid and
binding, X will have no cause of action. X
received $200. in consideration for his re-
lease. X's forbearance of his right to bring
a disputed claim against B is B's consideration.

(2) To avoid the release agreement:

(a) Argue that because X was in slight
shock and the agent knew about this after
speaking with the doctor, agent exerted *undue influence* on X to give up his claim. The
gross inadequacy of consideration relative
to the possibility of a tort claim may be presumptive evidence of this which it would
be B's burden to rebut. (Best chance on this
ground)

(b) Argue that agent was in a position of
trust with respect to X and thus the K was a
constructive fraud on X. Show that X knew

[*156*]

little of insurance matters and in his state of shock trusted the agent to be truthful. In this case full disclosure by the agent of the possibility of these injuries being serious and that large sums might be needed to be expended for them was necessary but not given. *But* the agent may have reasonably relied on the Doctor's opinion that X's injuries were minor so that the consideration was appropriate in the agent's eyes. (weaker ground for avoiding).

(c) Also argue that the agent's statement that "we will take care of any other expenses" was a misrepresentation of his present intention, that knowingly he falsely stated that in the future the Co. would take care of extra expenses. This would be difficult to prove.

If *avoided,* the Statute of Limitations may have run on the tort claim but argue that the agent's misrepresentation caused X to forbear from bringing suit while the statute ran and thus it should be no defense.

If *avoided* who may X sue? The agent, as disclosed agent, may be sued either for fraud or for negligently misrepresenting what the company would do. He may not be sued for the original tort claim since he was not a party to the accident.

B may be sued for fraud *or* for the original tort claim which neither the void agreement nor the Statute of Limitations will bar. (B may be sued for fraud because it is bound by the agent's actions).

The integration clause of the agreement will not operate to bar evidence of fraud or undue influence as evidence extrinsic to the writing in violation of the parol evidence rule. That rule operates only when it is shown that a written contract has been *freely entered into*. Extrinsic evidence of this nature does not contradict the terms of the K (as asserting that A promised X $300. instead of $200.) but merely shows that the contract did not exist in the first place because void on equitable principles.

.   .   .   .   .   .

COMMENT: Part (1) of this answer does not deal with the real issue involved: whether the Parol Evidence Rule and Integration clause preclude X from asserting Agent's promise to pay the first hospital bill. Part (2) discusses only a few of the possible bases for avoidance of the Release and brings in several matters of doubtful relevance to the facts given. Most instructors would not consider this a satisfactory answer and would grade it "D" at best.

CONTRACTS (II)

(one hour)

Piper, a physicist, had been employed for five years as head of the research staff of the Chemicon Co., which has its headquarters in New York City. During the previous two years he had demanded larger influence on the company's policy and though he owned only 400 shares of its stock had urged that he be elected to the board of directors. In particular he claimed that the company was unduly cautious in developing the cheaper methods of removing sulphur from fuel oil that Piper claimed to have invented. Finally Duffy, president of Chemicon, said to Piper in an acrimonious interview in Duffy's office: "You'll never find the money but if you think you're so great why don't you buy my shares?" Piper asked him to put this in writing. Duffy handed him a paper on which Duffy had written:

"If Peter Piper pays me $144,000 by certified check on or before May 20,

1970, I will sell him my entire holding in the Chemicon Co., 4800 shares, at the rate of $30 per share."

"Daniel Duffy"

The Chemicon Co. had issued 25,000 shares of stock, of which 4800 were owned by Duffy, a total of 11,000 were owned by five oil companies and the remaining 9200 were owned by 15 Chemicon employees (including Piper) in quantities ranging from 50 to 1200 shares. On May 15, 1970, Duffy was offered $38 a share for his Chemicon holdings by New York Jets, Inc., which had developed plans for a conglomerate merger that would absorb Chemicon. On Monday, May 18, Duffy learned to his amazement that Piper had succeeded in borrowing $200,000, that five junior executives of Chemicon had already sold and delivered to Piper the certificates for their Chemicon stock, totalling 2000 shares, and that Piper had already paid them the prices they had agreed to sell for, ranging from $32 to $35 a share. Early in the afternoon of Tuesday, May 19, Duffy flew to Bermuda and before leaving told his secretary, Miss Murphy, to communicate in no way with Piper and, if he called, to say that he (Duffy) had died that morning. Piper appeared at Duffy's office at 4:30 p. m.

on May 19 with a certified check for $144,-000 payable to Duffy in his pocket but when he appeared at the door was informed by Miss Murphy that Duffy had died that morning of a heart attack and that she had no authority to communicate with Piper in any way. That evening Piper placed the $144,-000 check in an envelope duly stamped and addressed to Duffy's office and mailed it in a New York City mailbox, where it remained for two weeks (because of a strike by New York City mail carriers which had begun on May 16). Duffy returned, much refreshed, from Bermuda on Monday, May 25, refused Piper's demand for the stock, and mailed the check back to Piper when it was finally delivered after the strike.

Write a concise opinion covering the issues, reasoning and probable conclusions as to Piper's rights and remedies and his chances of prevailing in an action against Duffy.

.   .   .   .   .   .

ANSWERS TO CONTRACTS (II)

GOOD "A" ANSWER

There may be a Statute of Frauds problem under the UCC, not § 2–201 dealing only with goods but in the article dealing with stock. In this case the statute would be complied with by Duffy's offer, it being "signed by the party to be charged" and expressing the parties, price, quantity and subject matter.

More importantly if an offer isn't made seriously, if the offeree knows this or a reasonable man in the offeree's position under the circumstances knows this, there can be no mutual assent and therefore no contractual obligation. Under the facts, however, there is little evidence to show that the offer wasn't made in seriousness even though made in the heat of argument, and there is no claim by the defendant, Duffy, that he was not serious. Even if he was not, there is no proof that Piper did not take him seriously. In fact the contrary seems certain since he went to the painstaking effort of buying out other holders and borrowing the money. Moreover, there is no evidence that a reasonable man in Piper's position would not have taken him seriously unless it was generally known that the stock was worth much more than $30. This cannot be assumed since Piper paid as low as $32 to get other stock. Even though the seriousness of an agreement is normally a question for the jury, (Chiles v. Good) there is little doubt in this case that (1) Piper thought the offer was serious, (2) so would a reasonable man. Under these circumstances Duffy's objective manifestations control, because Piper has acted in reliance on them, no matter what Duffy himself felt inside.

Even if it was a serious offer, it must have been accepted prior to termination. It is possible that if Duffy accepted the Jets' $38 price, this would be an attempted revocation prior to acceptance and if it was somehow communicated to Piper prior to his acceptance, this would generally constitute an effective revocation and terminate the contract. In the case of an option contract, this is not true, however, (Mier v. Hadden) provided there is consideration paid by the offeree to the offeror or at least purported to be paid (Rudolph, Restatement, Cochran v. Taylor). Although $1 is enough, in this case that wasn't even paid or promised so Duffy could probably have revoked. It is questionable whether Duffy even accepted the Jets' offer or, if so, that such acceptance was communicated to Piper, so there probably wasn't revocation.

The question, then, is whether Duffy through his secretary can revoke after Piper has tendered performance in a case where final performance necessitates acceptance of money by the offeror. The majority in Petterson v. Pattberg says the offeror can still revoke at that point while the minority says that there is acceptance by being ready, willing and able to pay. If the minority view prevails, there is arguably acceptance and a completed contract provided that Miss Murphy is an agent of Duffy authorized to accept the check. There is no doubt she is an agent, since Duffy has manifestly consented to have her act on his behalf in certain situations subject to his control. The question, however, is whether in accepting performance or being available for the tendering of performance she was exceeding her authority. There is no doubt that she had no actual authority to accept the check or its tender since she was specifically told not to. She may have had apparent authority since by placing her in the office Duffy manifested to Piper that she was available for this purpose, or she may have had inherent authority, which she probably did, to accept such a check since normally a secretary would have such authority, so that it wouldn't matter what Duffy told her.

But it is not clear that Piper actually tendered the check. If not, did the secretary as an agent of Duffy communicate revocation of the offer by telling Piper that Duffy was dead when Piper probably knew he wasn't? This is a close question, but I would say it would not constitute revocation even though actual death does terminate a contract when there is no option supported by consideration.

If as yet there was no acceptance or revocation, could Piper accept by mailing the check on May 19 even though it didn't arrive until two weeks after May 20. Normally in the U. S. acceptance occurs at the date of posting unless (1) the offer says otherwise, (2) the mail is delayed through a fault of the offeree, (3) the offeror impliedly authorizes a different means of acceptance by using that means in making his offer. In this case, Duffy wrote that Piper must pay him on or before May 20, so this may be explicitly commanding actual receipt by that date rather than mere posting. Second, if not, the mail wasn't delayed through the offeree's fault. That is, he couldn't end the mail strike. Yet, since it started three days prior to his mailing, he knew or should have known that his letter would probably be delayed unless the strike ended right away and therefore it probably was his fault that it didn't arrive within a reasonable time. Third, the means of communicating the offer was personal, so it could be said, as in Western Union v. Lucas, that the means of communicating acceptance must be the same. Yet, this was not possible since Duffy left town, so using the Henthorn v. Fraser approach, Duffy could have expected acceptance by letter. However, at the time of making the offer, Duffy couldn't anticipate leaving so this may cause this case to vary from Henthorn. Thus, it seems that for one of these three reasons, acceptance at this point wasn't made prior to May 20.

If there was acceptance at any of these points this would be a completed contract, and Duffy would have to transfer his stock. Since he refused, there would be a breach, since there were concurrent conditions but Piper had arguably tendered performance.

In this case there are two possible remedies. The first is in damages. Under this remedy Piper can recover for damages suffered that the parties had reason to anticipate at the time the contract was made, provided they can be measured in money terms with reasonable certainty. In this case, they may be what Duffy was offered by N.Y. Jets or what Piper paid for the other stock plus the interest on his borrowing money to pay for the stock minus his expenses saved which was the $144,000. However, this would not give him the large interest he wanted so that he could have a major influence on the company and the other holders may be unwilling to sell for any price so that damages wouldn't be an adequate remedy at law. In such case, he should be entitled to specific performance provided it is equitable and practical to order and feasible to enforce. In Armstrong v. Stiffler it was said it is equitable even if the offeree received a controlling interest so it would certainly be equitable in this situation. It would also be feasible if the stock wasn't already sold to N.Y. Jets as a Bona Fide purchaser, although a receiver may have to be appointed to complete the transaction. Therefore specific performance should be granted, provided again that there was acceptance of the offer which is debatable.

. . . . . .

COMMENT: This answer deals with most of the issues of offer-acceptance and remedies-

for-breach involved in the problem. It is well-written, refers to the rules and cases applicable to the issues, presents good analyses and arguments as to their application to the facts, and states the probable conclusions asked for at the end of the problem.

MARGINAL ANSWER

(a) Promises must be seriously given or seriously understood before they can be binding. If the offer by Duffy was intended and understood as a joke, or mere "breast-beating" by Duffy, no power of acceptance could be created because he would not be understood to be offering anything; and the parties would be assenting to something not intended. If, however, Duffy meant it seriously and Piper understood it as being a serious offer, a power of acceptance would be created.

Duffy might say that Piper did not take it seriously but in good faith attempted to say he did when he learned of the Jet's offer to him. Piper might say he took it seriously and try to show that he knew of the Jet's offer and should have warned him. However, Duffy has the burden of proof in this situation.

(b) Was the power of acceptance created and did Piper accept so as to make a binding K?

The secretary can only act as agent to bind Duffy within the scope of his consent which he specifically withdrew in regards to dealing with Duffy. So she could not accept Piper's tender of his performance and tender to her did not operate as receipt of acceptance by Duffy.

Death usually terminates an offer whether or not offeree has notice but in this case Duffy did not die but in bad faith communicated to Piper that he did. Offer still open, but not accepted.

Usually an acceptance is effective upon mailing but here was not effective because it was stipulated that Piper must pay Duffy to make the offer effective. Offer was not accepted by mailing.

Duffy's receipt of the check after May 20 when the offer had expired was too late but Duffy caused the delay by his evasive actions, so one could argue that Piper's attempted tender was valid and binding on Duffy.

[*169*]

(c) But was the offer revoked?

It may be argued that Duffy's actions indicated to Piper that he was revoking the offer and that therefore the power of acceptance was terminated. Most likely even though Duffy did cause the delay of the acceptance, Piper should have understood that Duffy was revoking.

Although stated in terms of an option K, not even nominal consideration was given and Duffy may revoke.

But even though an offer as a gratuitous promise is freely revocable, Duffy's attempted revocation was after Piper had relied upon his promise and was substantially prejudiced.

Although Piper may not sue for loss of bargain (the difference between the $30. per share in the offer and the $38. offered by the N. Y. Jets) he could recover reliance damages, if he has any. In this case, the profit he could make on his own stock and that of the other employees might cover the cost of the loan. If not, Duffy will have to reimburse him for the difference.

.   .   .   .   .   .

COMMENT: A comparison of this answer with the preceding "A" answer shows clearly the numerous relevant issues not dealt with here, the much more disjointed and superficial analysis of those here discussed, and why this answer is only marginally adequate if that.

AGENCY (IN CONTRACT CASES)

(one hour)

O owned and operated a cafe in Minneapolis. He also owned a cafe in Duluth and hired M as general manager for it. O told M that M was to hire such employees as he needed, purchase necessary food and supplies and do such other things as were necessary to operate the cafe in accordance with O's management policies, which O explained to M. O opened a checking account in B bank in Duluth in the name of "O Cafe", and gave B Bank M's signature and written instructions that M was "authorized to sign checks for cafe purposes, and to indorse and deposit checks and drafts payable to the O Cafe." Not long after M began operating the cafe, F, a member of the Duluth Policemen's Association, came in and asked M to buy a $50 advertisement in a souvenir program for a benefit show being put on for the Policemen's Pension Fund. O had told M that "we build business through good food and service" but had said nothing specific about advertising. In fact, O never advertised, but neither M nor F knew this. M decided that taking an ad would be a good thing for the business and signed a slip "O Cafe, M Manager" which provided that O Cafe would pay the Association $50 for an ad, the terms of which M wrote on the slip. Later that week O was in Duluth and when M told O about the ad O became angry, said that this was utterly contrary to his business policies, that he also hated cops and that he would not pay for the ad. O ordered M out of the cafe, telling him he was fired and refusing to pay him. This made M mad. While getting his things from the cafe office he took one of the cafe check forms which he later filled out, making it payable to himself for the amount of his current month's salary, and signing it as he signed other checks for cafe purposes. This he cashed at B bank which had not yet learned of his discharge. O refused to pay for the ad, and when he learned about the check, he demanded that the Bank reimburse his account in that amount. The Bank refused.

(a) Is O liable to the Policemen's Association for the $50 ad (assuming the ad was published as ordered by M)?

(b) Can O recover the amount of the check from B Bank?

(c) What, if any, rights has the Policemen's Association against M if O should be held not liable for the ad?

.   .   .   .   .   .

ANSWERS TO AGENCY

GOOD "A" ANSWER

(a) Yes, O *is* liable to the Policemen's Association for the $50 ad. It is true that O did not *expressly* authorize M to buy ads, and it is quite obvious that O did *not* in any way "ratify" the deal between M and F after he learned about it. However, there are three other bases on which O could be held liable to the Policemen's Association. These are "Implied Actual Authority", "Apparent Authority" and "Inherent Agency Power".

Certainly O hired M as his general agent and, in permitting M to operate the cafe, also "held M out" and "clothed" him with all the appearances of such an agent. In giving M express authority to operate the cafe, O gave M actual *implied* authority, and also "apparent authority" as to third persons, to do all those things a cafe manager with a business bank account would ordinarily be authorized and expected to do in operating a cafe. Such things would also be within M's "Inherent Agency Power" to bind O.

Whether O is liable to the Policeman's Association thus depends upon whether contracting for the ad was an act reasonably and ordinarily incidental to and within the "ordinary scope" of a cafe manager's employment.

It is true that O never advertised, but M was not told this, and certainly F did not know it. It does not seem unreasonable at all to assume that a restaurant manager would have the desire, implied authority, and even the responsibility to advertise the business and maintain good relations with the police. Even if it were determined that M, in view of what O had told him about O's policies, could not reasonably imply O's actual consent to advertising and thus did not have actual *implied* authority to contract for the ad, he could still have "Apparent Authority" and "Inherent Agency Power" to do it since M's buying a simple, $50 ad under these circumstances would reasonably appear to be within the ordinary scope of his employment as a cafe manager. Thus, I believe that O *is* bound to pay the $50 to the Policemen's Association.

(b) No, O can not recover the amount of the check from B bank.

O had instructed the Bank that M was authorized to indorse checks which were payable to "O Cafe." The check in question was drawn by and made payable to M, and thus the Bank was not authorized to pay it under that instruction from O. However, O had also instructed the Bank that M was to have authority to draw and sign checks on the account "for cafe purposes." It was arguably reasonable for the bank to assume that drawing a check to pay the cafe manager's salary was a valid "cafe purpose."

Thus, the Bank was probably acting within the express limitations which O had prescribed in paying this check.

Also, since M was arguably acting within what would be the ordinary scope of the job of a manager (seeing that all salaries, including his own, were paid), M was acting within the apparent scope of his agency.

It is true, of course, that M had been discharged and was no longer O's agent with any actual authority. But O still can not recover the amount of the check from the bank because M still had "Apparent Authority" as to the bank. A principal continues to be liable for the acts of a discharged agent, within the scope of his agency, as to third parties with whom he has dealt, until the third parties learn of his discharge. His Apparent Authority as to such third parties continues although his agency and Actual Authority end.

The fact that M's act was solely for his *own* benefit does not matter if the Bank had no notice of this. A principal is liable to innocent third parties for the acts of his agent within his "Apparent Authority" even though the agent's acts are actually fraudulent toward the principal and totally self-serving and unauthorized.

(c) If it should be found by a court that O was *not* liable on any basis for the $50 ad, the Association's only recourse would be against M, who could be held liable for the damages to the Association caused by not getting O's obligation.

Since M would not have been acting as an authorized agent of O, M's deal with the Association could be actionable in tort as fraud if M knew, or was negligent in not knowing, that his purchase of the ad was not authorized or within the scope of his job. On this basis M would be liable for the Association's actual damages. Even if M contracted for the ad in the good faith and reasonable belief that he was authorized to do so and was thus not guilty of tortious misrepresentation, he could be liable to the Association for actual damages (out-of-pocket loss) on the basis of a breach of the Implied Warranty of Authority that agents are deemed to make to third parties who rely upon the agents' assumption of authority.

The "contract" between the Association and O (made by M for O) for the ad purported to be solely between the "O Cafe" and the Association. M signed only as "Manager" and not as a contracting party, and thus is not obligated to pay the $50 contract price even if O was not bound and is not liable for it. M's liability is for the Association's *damages* (e. g. cost of the ad and other out-of-pocket expense) not for any promised expectancy under the contract.

．　　　．　　　．　　　．　　　．

MARGINAL ANSWER

(a) O may be liable to the Policemen's Association when one looks to M as having apparent authority.

If a principal (O in this case) clothes his agent (M) as having apparent authority through O's conduct or words so as to make the third party reasonably certain that M has the authority, then this may make O liable for the damage ($50).

One would have to look at whether O did conduct himself as to whether or not to give

F the impression that M did have the authority. I think one walking into a cafe and talking to the manager as to this ad deal could possibly give one the impression that M did have the authority.

If we look to the *Watteau* case, there the principal was liable for the acts of it's agent, because the agent was buying cigars etc. which would normally be within the scope of his employment. Also there the principal was undisclosed, as was also the situation in this case. Going by *Watteau* I think O would possibly be liable because M was only performing the duties that normally go with a job such as this.

O's counter argument would be the *Levi* v. *Booth* case. The rule there was that just because one normally carries on with the selling of jewelry in that case, does not give the agent apparent authority.

The UCC has basically overruled the *Levi* case, however, and states that such an agent would be liable to an innocent buyer.

It possibly could be argued that the Police Association could not recover from O, because O has pointed out to M what his limitations were, and M in going beyond his duty should be the only one liable for any damages that occurred.

However here the *Watteau* case would overrule this argument. Under it, O would be liable despite any secret limitation put on M, as long as M performed his duty as is normally done with such a job.

It may be argued that the Police Association cannot recover from O because O did not ratify the agreement made between M and F.

(b) O may not be able to recover from the bank because the Bank was given to understand, by the actions and words of O, that M had the right to use the checking account in connection with the cafe.

The *Livingston* case points out that when one is given apparent authority, as here, to perform an act, then the principal would incur the loss if such act is done.

At the time of the act of M in cashing the check he no longer had the authority to do so. So in reality the bank no longer had a right to give him the money.

But the bank could in no way know that M did not have the authority to cash the check. And when one (bank) is under the impression that M is still the agent of O, because of lack of notification to the contrary by O, then the bank would not be liable. This is brought out in the *Courtney* case.

O may say that M was fraudulent in cashing the check, and therefore the bank should be liable to him because of an illegal transaction. This argument doesn't stand up when we consider that as long as one is made to believe through the acts of the principal (O) that the bank has legal authority, we cannot pass over it and make such illegal later. Pointed out in the *Blue Sky Law* case. *Bangor* case says one who settles in good faith cannot be liable again, so here O should not be.

(c) M may be able to recover from O if not from M. Since the principal (O) was undisclosed, and M was acting without authority in his own name, and O did not later ratify the agreement, then only A should be liable.

One would have to consider whether M was acting in his own name only, however, or if signing the slip in the name of "O Cafe" constituted a disclosure to F as to who M's principal was. One would need more time to better ascertain the facts to decide this.

If the agreement was made and signed in a way to disclose to F the principal, O, then the Association may have a cause of action against O.

[*181*]

As brought out in the *Kelly Asphalt* case, if the agent M makes no claim as to who the real principal is and does not fraudulently claim to be the principal, then the Police Association could only have a cause of action against O if O would later ratify the agreement. But this case can be differentiated.

Kline indicates that the Police Association would not have a cause of action against O unless he later ratified the contract, especially when M went beyond his authority.

.   .   .   .   .   .

COMMENT: This answer, although as long as the "A" answer, is typical of numerous poor or marginal answers. The writer recognizes in a general way the main and obvious issues involved in the problem and the cases that may be relevant in deciding them, but his understanding of both is limited, confused and inaccurate. Furthermore he has not developed even a minimum degree of professional skill in formulating and expressing rules, reasons or arguments in writing. His statements are neither clear nor wholly accurate so that what he writes is ambiguous and difficult to follow at many points. In short, the answer is very poorly written and

leaves the impression that he really doesn't understand either the law or its application. As a result, this would be considered an "F" answer by some instructors and no better than a marginal "D" by most.

TORTS

GENERAL COMMENT: Torts, like Contracts, is a broad, major division in the Private Law—Civil-Liability area but is less unified. It includes a number of distinct types of private legal wrongs with different elements of liability, such as the various intentional torts of Assault, Battery, False Imprisonment, Deceit, Defamation and others, plus the broader categories of "Negligence" and "Strict Liability." Examination problems in Torts thus will contain facts that may involve any one or more of these torts and require analyses of the particular elements of liability for, and possible defenses to, each tort that may have been committed.

Sometimes torts exam problems will involve fairly simple, two-party situations with only a few possibilities and issues. It is increasingly common, however, for examiners to give fewer problems with fairly long and complex fact situations involving numerous parties, questions and issues which reflect the expanding thrust of tort liability in our ever more complex, urbanized and mechanized society with its multiple hazards. The three problems below illustrate these more complicated situations and problems you are likely to encounter in a Torts exam.

.   .   .   .   .   .

TORTS (I)

(one and one-quarter hours)

You are an associate in the law firm of Garratt, Cucinotti, Slocum and Bud. You have received the following memorandum from Vittorio Cucinotti, one of the senior partners. Prepare an answering memorandum for Mr. Cucinotti, in compliance with the instructions contained in his memorandum.

MEMORANDUM

FROM: V. Cucinotti   Dated June 7, 1971

TO: Associate

We have been retained by Mrs. Faith Eternal and her husband, Ernest, to bring suits on their behalf against various persons connected with a series of horrendous experiences recently suffered by the Eternals at All Souls Hospital. The story told to us by the Eternals is as follows:

On June 1, 1970, Faith and her husband reported to All Souls Hospital pursuant to prior arrangements made by Faith's obstetrician,

Dr. Josiah Black. Faith was to give birth, by Caesarean section, to her first child. After prior consultation with Faith and Ernest, Dr. Black had arranged for the Caesarean to be performed on June 3, 1970, at 11:00 a. m. by Dr. Alfonso White, chief of surgery at All Souls.

Upon arrival at the hospital, Ernest and Faith filled out the necessary forms in the admitting office. Among other things, they indicated that they had no hospitalization insurance; and they both signed a printed form which read:

> "We, Ernest Eternal and Faith Eternal (being husband and wife), hereby consent to the performance of a Caesarean section on Faith Eternal. We understand that a Caesarean section is the surgical procedure of taking a child from the uterus by cutting through the walls of the abdomen and uterus. We further consent to the surgical repair of any organs related to the operation, which the surgeon, in his professional judgment, deems appropriate for the adequate protection of the patient's health.
>
> Dated: June 1, 1970.
>
> /s/ Ernest Eternal
>
> /s/ Faith Eternal"

[186]

On the evening of her first day in the hospital, Faith was visited by a man in a white jacket with a stethoscope around his neck. She assumed he was a physician on the hospital staff. Actually, he was Oscar Potfull, a hospital orderly. Oscar has the intelligence of a nine-year old child. He is perfectly competent at performing the usual clean-up duties of a hospital orderly, but he likes to pretend he is a doctor. In fact, while he is pretending he is a doctor, he believes in good faith that he is a doctor and that he heals the sick. He has never harmed a patient; he merely enjoys listening to their heartbeats with his stethoscope. Oscar asked Faith how she was feeling and told her he was there to give her a brief examination. Faith sat up in bed. Oscar put the stethoscope in his ears, and was about to apply the other end of the stethoscope to Faith's chest, when something about his manner indicated to Faith that he was not a physician. She screamed. A passing nurse came into the room, saw Potfull, and persuaded him to leave. Faith was in a nervous condition as a result of the experience. Involuntary shudders ran up and down her spine; she perspired heavily; and she was given a sedative to help her sleep.

Dr. Black decided it would be better for Faith to be operated on at 9:00 a. m. on June 3, 1970 than at the originally scheduled 11:00 a. m.   He so advised the surgical scheduling office of the hospital.   The operating room had been reserved for a Caesarean to be performed at 9:00 a. m. by Drs. John Smith and William Jones on a Mrs. Wilma Adams.   The surgical scheduling office, pursuant to Dr. Black's request, rescheduled Faith for her Caesarean at 9:00 a. m. (the time originally arranged for Mrs. Adams) and rescheduled Mrs. Adams for her Caesarean at 11:00 a. m. (the time originally arranged for Faith). But, the surgical planning office failed to inform Drs. White, Smith and Jones of the switch.

At 8:45 a. m. on June 3, 1970, Faith was wheeled into the operating room and was given general anesthesia rendering her totally unconscious.   At 9:00 a. m. Drs. Smith and Jones reported to the operating room to perform the Caesarean on Mrs. Adams.   As it turns out, Mrs. Adams bears a striking resemblance to Faith Eternal, and Drs. Smith and Jones went ahead with the operation on Faith, in the good faith belief they were working on Mrs. Adams.   They delivered a bouncing baby girl (whom the Eternals have named Hope) 9 pounds, 10 ounces. While the incision was open Drs. Jones and Smith noticed a "window" in the uterus. A "window" is a weakness in the wall of the uterus which creates the risk of rupture during pregnancy. It can be surgically repaired, or the fallopian tubes can be tied off so as to prevent conception and future pregnancy. Dr. Smith went to the waiting room and explained the condition to Mr. Adams, (whom Smith thought to be the husband of the patient). Since Mrs. Adams already had 2 children (to whom she had given normal birth) he recommended that the tubes be tied off, and Mr. Adams agreed. Dr. Smith then returned to the operating room and tied off Faith's tubes.

On June 10, 1970, Dr. Black informed Faith and Ernest that Faith and her new baby could leave the hospital at 10:00 a. m. on June 11, 1970. He told Earnest that he would sign and deliver a release slip to the admitting office, and that Earnest should stop at the admitting office the following morning upon his arrival at the hospital. At 9:30 a. m. on June 11, 1970, Ernest reported to the admitting office. Mr. Clarence Williams, supervisor of the office, told Ernest that his hospital bill totalled $1,000.00, and inasmuch as Ernest had no hospitalization insurance, it

[*189*]

would be necessary for Ernest to pay the bill before Faith or the baby would be permitted to leave the hospital. Ernest told Williams he only had $500 in his checking account and would raise and pay the balance of the bill the following week. Williams insisted that the bill had to be paid in full before Faith or the baby could leave the hospital. Ernest stayed and argued with Williams in an attempt to persuade Williams to change his mind. 10.00 a. m. came and went and Ernest did not show up at Faith's room to take her home. She became increasingly nervous and asked the nurse to check on his whereabouts. The nurse reported back that Ernest was having some difficulty in the admitting office. Finally, at 12:00 o'clock noon, Ernest persuaded Williams to accept the $500 on account and wait for the balance of $500. Ernest then picked up Faith and the baby and took them home.

All Souls is a non-profit institution, but, as you know, it does not enjoy charitable immunity under the laws of this jurisdiction.

I have determined that we will institute suits on behalf of Faith against:

    1. The hospital, for the conduct of Potfull,

2. Dr. Jones for battery,

3. Dr. Smith for battery.

We will also institute suit on behalf of Ernest against Mr. Williams and the hospital for false imprisonment.

Please prepare a memorandum informing me of your opinion as to whether the above-mentioned suits are likely to be successful. Indicate in each instance the essential elements of the cause of action, what we will have to prove, the defenses likely to be raised, and what arguments we can use to avoid any such defenses.

.   .   .   .   .   .

COMMENT: The fact that instructors who prepare exam problems sometimes, as in the foregoing problem, exercise their sense of humor or whimsy in selecting names for the parties, or even propound what seem to be "far-out" fact situations, should not lead you to take such problems lightly or to conclude that they are not "realistic" or "practical". An exploration of reported cases will often disclose actual names and occurrences more bizarre and sometimes more ridiculous or horrendous than anything an imaginative examiner could dream up. Truth is often

stranger than fiction, so enjoy a chuckle when one of these is encountered and then deal with it thoroughly and seriously.

.   .   .   .   .   .

ANSWERS TO TORTS (I)

GOOD "A" ANSWER

1. Faith v. Hospital.

A. The action against the hospital for Potfull's conduct would have to be based upon the Agency principle of respondeat superior. An employer is liable for the tortious acts of his servant if done within the scope of the servant's employment. Even though Potfull was apparently in the general process of going about his normal duties when he approached Faith, the question of "scope" would turn on whether or not his "detour" from duty was within a "permissible" or "foreseeable" zone of deviation. This is a standard followed by many courts and seems to be the best test.

Applying this test, it would seem that the deviation was "foreseeable" and thus within "scope" in view of the fact that his hospital supervisor was undoubtedly aware of Potfull's mental retardation and his going around with a stethoscope.

B. Theory of recovery:

The most likely theory of recovery would probably be assault. Battery wouldn't apply because there was no contact with Faith. Intentional infliction of mental anguish wouldn't apply because Potfull obviously meant no harm. Also Faith's nervous condition was not severe enough. Mere fright and difficulty in sleeping has been held not to be severe enough for this tort.

The elements of assault which we, on plaintiff's behalf, would have to establish would be:

1) A volitional act by defendant. This is clearly met as Potfull acted volitionally;

2) Intent to touch. This is met as Potfull did intend to touch Faith. (Malice isn't necessary);

3) Apprehension of an immediate harmful or offensive contact. This element is met since Faith knew that Potfull was about to make an intimate examination of her body. The offensiveness requirement can be met by an affront to plaintiff's dignity and that can be found in these circumstances where her breast would be bared to Potfull.

4) Causation—the threatened touching must be by the defendant or by a force set in motion by him. The tort is complete at this point. Actual damages need be proved only for extra recovery.

5) Lack of consent—Plaintiff did at first consent but this was procured by Potfull's fraud and wouldn't be a defense. Thus, the hospital could be held liable to Faith.

2. Faith v. Drs. Jones and Smith for battery.

The elements which plaintiff would have to establish for a prima facie case of battery would be:

1) A volitional act by the defendants;

2) Intent to touch;

3) Harmful or offensive contact;

4) Causation;

5) Lack of plaintiff's consent.

Defendants could argue that they did not intend to operate on plaintiff. However, this would be an example of "transferred intent". If X intends to strike A but hits B instead, he is still liable for battery on B. Defendants acted volitionally, not unconsciously

The next problem is whether or not there was a harmful or offensive contact. Any alteration of the body's function or organs is considered a harmful contact, so the necessary contact could be established here.

There is no problem with causation since the harmful contact was directly caused by the defendants in performing the operation. The defendants' main argument will probably be that plaintiff consented to the operation. Faith's signed consent statement did not limit the operation to any specific doctor. The defendants might argue therefore that since the plaintiffs had consented orally to have the operation performed by a surgeon other than their own obstetrician there was implied consent to the operation performed by defendants. Furthermore, they will probably argue that they went ahead in good faith and that there was no mistake in the type of operation performed and no negligence on their part in operating.

These arguments will probably be rejected because the court would probably give effect to the orally expressed intentions of the plaintiff as to her surgeon, in addition to the written consent in the hospital form.

I think that both Dr. Jones and Dr. Smith would be liable for battery on these facts. Even if Dr. Jones isn't found liable, Dr. Smith will be liable for tying off the tubes.

Assuming that the court did find implied consent for the Caesarean delivery by defendants, such consent could not be found for any extension of the operation which exceeded the original consent.

Defendants will, of course, argue that the written consent expressly allowed any extension related to the operation. This is a good argument but the plaintiff can meet it by arguing that the defendants evidently didn't consider this a related extension since one went to the waiting room to ask for consent from Faith's supposed husband.

The consent by the wrong husband, who already had two children, cannot be binding on Faith or be assumed to be immaterial to her since this was her first child.

3. Ernest v. Williams and Hospital for false imprisonment.

The elements which the plaintiff will have to establish for false imprisonment are:

    1) A volitional act by defendant;

    2) Intent to confine plaintiff;

    3) Actual confinement to a defined area;

    4) Causation;

    5) Lack of consent by plaintiff. The action against the hospital would have to be

based upon respondeat superior (previously discussed). Williams was definitely acting within the scope of his employment so the doctrine applies here. I do not think that plaintiff can establish his case.

First of all it appears that there was no intent to confine plaintiff. Williams did not say that plaintiff could not leave. Only Faith and Hope were confined by delay in release.

Secondly there was no confinement of plaintiff to a defined area. Confinement can be by words, conduct, threats or by actual physical barriers, but there must be actual confinement. Other elements thus need not be discussed.

.   .   .   .   .   .

COMMENT: A very well organized, well-written answer to the precise questions asked in the problem, covering practically all of the issues that could properly be raised on the facts in concise, well-reasoned arguments in support of the conclusions reached. Probably would get the top grade from most instructors.

MARGINAL ANSWER

A. Suits on behalf of Faith

1) Faith v. Hospital:

Utilizing the concept of Respondeat Superior the hospital is clearly responsible for the adequate control of its personnel in securing the safety of its patients. A cause of action against the hospital would include the following elements:

a) Potfull was an actual employee of the hospital and could be held as primarily negligent if Potfull acted substantially outside the scope of his duties since the socially secured interest—patient's physical and mental well-being is socially protected by law.

i) Clearly the hospital has a DUTY to see its employees are fit for their work and to prevent foreseeable occasions as the instant case.

ii) This DUTY should be protected by a standard of conduct hospitals generally adhere to in the mental makeup of employees which might result in patient injury, etc. This standard can be derived from hospital administration journals, administration and practice. Also, since this touches on an area where no special medical knowledge is needed to make a justifiable inference, a jury, utilizing common knowledge, and a "reasonable man" standard composed of communal standards and their own experience, could also come to a decision about the hospital's due care or lack of it.

b) It would have to be established that the hospital had actual or constructive knowledge of Potfull's behavior. Then it would have to be decided whether the probability and gravity of any possible harm he might have done was justified because of the economic utility in retaining him.

c) Next we will have to prove that Potfull's behavior was the proximate cause of the nervous disorder, a fact which should be obtainable from the medical records and nurses (Faith was pregnant so probably closely watched). This should be feasible.

d) Breach of the hospital's standard of care should be proven by recourse to (see a) i) common knowledge ii) hospital administration procedure generally.

e) Lastly, the "nervous disorder" is a compensable injury, i. e. the tort law recognizes it since there is apparently a "physical coloration" or hook involved—nervous system as a physiological structure—that is, there has been a negligent invasion of the bodily dignity which the law believes measurable, not liable to sham, and hence is financially amenable to recovery.

The *hospital defenses* would include the following:

a) In light of the apparent danger, the hospital acted reasonably in gainfully employing Potfull and carefully guarded his activities.

b) Proof to the effect that the hospital generally employs persons of Potfull's mental caliber for valid economic and humanitarian reasons and to allow recovery here would negate this important social policy.

c) No real damage was done and the nurse fulfilled the due care standard by her prompt attention to the action.

d) Since the hospital was not negligent (above) in the performance of its duties no strict liability theory should be applied.

e) The defense would also include an impressive array of nurses and doctors attesting to the basically harmless nature of Potfull.

f) Assumption of risk.

In *responding to these defenses* we would say:

a) The wronged patient should not bear the burden of a wrong—that if the hospital wants to act "humanely" it should bear the burden or get the state to.

b) The patient does not consciously assume the risk of a mentally deficient employee. No alternative to the hospital.

c) The hospital was negligent (basic element in case).

d) Finally, if anyone is to bear the unfortunate loss it should be a third party—insurance or state—which the hospital should foresee and protect itself with since sovereign immunity no longer applies.

2) Faith v. Drs. Jones and Smith for battery.

a) Permission for Smith and Jones to operate and touch the body arose only insofar as they (c/a elements):

1) received consent (tort defense to what otherwise would be battery) from the patient, and

2) to the extent agreed upon.

b) the waiver that Ernest and Faith signed does not apply to Smith and Jones. No privity of contract and in a highly personal service of this type the court surely would not extend consent beyond the original parties. Hence, any argument by the doctors using this waiver would fail.

c) In attempting such a drastic surgical procedure, Smith and Jones should be held to a very high standard of care and it should be feasible to prove negligence in light of the fact that they do not seem to recognize their patients' external or internal person. Certainly a standard of care would, at the minimum, involve a positive identification, visual, X-rays.

Of course the doctors would say the resemblance was so great that they did not think of taking more adequate precautions about identifying their patient. Nevertheless, we seem to be in an area where laymen can rightly judge and expect extreme care on a surgeon's part. Certainly, at the least, it would be a jury question as to whether Smith and Jones failed to exercise due care as far as i) getting permission, ii) checking to see if right patient, not merely using visual laymen means but by medical criteria,

i. e. temperature, blood pressure, physiological makeup.

d) the doctors will try to avoid liability by blaming the surgical planning office which co-authored, as it were, the wrong. The surgical planning was a "concurrent cause" in the battery and also breached their duties. Nevertheless, although both parties may have contributed to the result by their negligence, they both can be held liable. As against the innocent victim, both had a duty and standard of conduct which can be shown to have been breached.

e) Assumption of Risk—a patient, unconscious in surgery, cannot be said to voluntarily assume the risk of activities which must practically be left to the careful, skilled hands of surgeons and hospital staff.

f) Contributory negligence is not present since Faith did not act "unreasonably in any way".

In short, a strong case, given more research and facts, should be able to be built against Smith and Jones. I do not believe they can evade liability by pleading they were merely agents of the hospital—for surgeons there should be some non-delegable aspect of due care.

B. Ernest v. Mr. Williams for false imprisonment.

Elements: 1) Ernest and Faith were confined against their will for an appreciable length of time, i. e. 9:30 A.M. to 12:00 o'clock

2) Because of Faith's condition he could not use any force to get her out and she had, obviously, no egress open to her. In such a situation a plaintiff is not obligated to suffer physical force or social embarrassment to avoid imprisonment

3) Williams intended to keep them there, perhaps from ill will or economic motives, since they previously had informed him about their financial condition.

4) The plaintiffs knew of Williams' intent to confine and Faith in fact had nervous difficulties because of it.

In defense Williams will probably say he was privileged, i. e. standard operating procedure to secure a reasonable economic agreement before letting the patient leave. In addition, he was not negligent in doing so, not abusive.

Patients who do not have insurance "assume the risk".

Williams was merely an agent of the hospital and didn't know about their signature attesting to that fact.

All these arguments seem to be of a flimsy nature and given the elements as delineated above and the availability of proof, they should be rebuttable.

Patients do not "Assume the risk" of abuse because of lack of insurance. The hospital and Williams both could be liable for his wrong doing. His interest did not warrant his action given the emotional state of Faith. Recovery should be possible against Williams (and maybe the hospital).

. . . . . .

COMMENT: This answer is organized, and adequately written in part A, but contains numerous errors and irrelevancies. In A(1) the doctrine of vicarious liability under respondeat superior is confused with the responsibility of an employer for his own negligence in supervising employees. No facts are given justifying the extensive discussion of the hospital's negligence and defenses. The analysis of "nervous disorder" as compensable injury is very confused. In A(2), where

the memorandum requests an opinion as to actions "for battery" the writer discusses the negligence of the doctors, plaintiff's assumption of risk and contributory negligence; discussions not requested by the senior partner and thus not relevant to the problem or facts. In B, the discussion deals with the rights and situation of Faith as a co-plaintiff with Ernest, when that is not asked for and the situations of the two were quite different. Ernest was in no way confined; Faith was but didn't know about it. The elements of false imprisonment are not carefully or accurately analyzed or applied to Ernest as requested. This (B) answer is disjointed, confusing and poorly written. The language is flowery but simply not used in a manner to convey clear meaning or coherent thought. This would be no better than a "D" paper. Some would grade it "F".

TORTS (II)

(One Hour)

Archer, Ltd., manufactured a patented geared transmission for use on bicycles, which it sold to a number of manufacturers of cycles in America and Europe. Archer advertised in *Life* Magazine as follows:

"FLY WITH AN ARCHER GEARED
TRANSMISSION"

"The Finest in the World"

"Our never-fail transmission will carry you effortlessly over hill and dale with only the slightest effort on your part.

"Just a flick of the lever and you move smoothly from high to low and then back again into high!

Remember to look for the Archer

on fine cycles everywhere!"

The "archer" symbol appears on the transmission and the gear shift lever.

Byke Company purchased Archer Geared Transmissions for installation on the bicycles which it manufactured. The geared trans-

mission was installed by Byke's employees
in the rear wheel assembly, with the gear
shift lever and cable attached to the transmission, not to the handlebars or frame.
The dis-assembled bicycle (including frame,
front and rear wheel assemblies, drive chain,
pedals, seat, handlebars and instructions for
assembly and adjustment of brakes, gears,
handle bars, seats, etc.) was then crated for
shipment to purchasers who were expected
to assemble the bicycle according to the en-
closed instructions.

Coast-to-Coast Cycle Shops, Inc., purchased crated bicycles from Byke Co. which
it sold in its stores throughout the country
as "COASTAR" a name appearing on a label
affixed to the frame by decal over the original words "Byke Special" but leaving un-
covered "built by Byke Company". The assembly of each bicycle and affixing of the
"Coastar" label occurred in each of the individual shops or stores owned and operated
by Coast-to-Coast. The relabelling was done
with the specific permission of Byke Co.
under a contract for sale in which Coast-to-
Coast agreed to waive all warranties on the
part of Byke Co.

Father purchased a "Coastar" as a graduation present for Diana, his 17 year old
daughter. After inquiring whether the bi-

cycle would be delivered in "full working order" and being assured that "The Coastar is fully assembled and ready to go," he made full payment of the purchase price and had the "Coastar" delivered to his home for presentation on graduation night.

The following weekend, Diana was cycling on her new "Coastar" with some of her friends on a country roadway. Edward, aged 18, who was one of the group, challenged Diana to a race. About midway in the "course" of the race there was a long steep hill. Halfway up the hill, Diana stood up on the pedals to pump harder and shifted from the next-lowest to the lowest gear position with the gear shift lever. The transmission suddenly disengaged, causing the pedals to move very freely. Diana was caught off-balance by the sudden movement of the pedals and pitched sideways. Edward, who had seen Diana rise on the pedals and shift down, had begun to cut her off by turning across her projected path of travel. At the point where the gear transmission disengaged and Diana lost her balance, Edward was "neck and neck" with her bicycle. Diana's "Coastar" fell against Edward's bicycle and both were thrown to the ground.

Diana suffered severe lacerations and a broken leg as a result of the fall on the two cycles. Edward, who fell away from the cycles suffered some lacerations and a broken arm. Both cycles were damaged and required repair.

Discuss: (1) Diana's claims for damages against (a) Archer Ltd., (b) Byke Co., and (c) Coast-to-Coast Cycle Shops, Inc.; and (2) Edward's claims for damages against Coast-to-Coast Shops Inc. Indicate in your discussion all the alternative claims or theories which may be made, how each claim or theory must be supported or proved and the difficulties of establishing each claim. Assume that the jurisdiction in which these claims will be litigated has no prior decisions which are binding on the courts which will decide the claims, but that the court will apply general principles of tort law.

.   .   .   .   .   .

COMMENT: This type of exam problem so bristles with possible issues, both substantive and procedural, conflicting theories of legal liability, multiple parties and fact-analyses, that no one could possibly deal adequately with all aspects of it in the time normally available in a law examination. The examiner's purpose is to see how many of these questions in this common-but-complex type

of problem each student can recognize and how well they can be analyzed, reasoned through and stated. **The following answers illustrate substantial differences in scope and depth of treatment.**

ANSWERS TO TORTS (II)

GOOD "A" ANSWER

The factual situation presented represents essentially two separate causes of action arising from the same transaction or occurrence: the claim of Diana against multiple defendants and Edward's claim against the bicycle assembler and distributor, Coast to Coast.

The action involved presents a question of product liability as directed to 3 separate defendants, each of whom was involved in production of the instrumentality producing Diana and Edward's injuries.

This answer will first consider Diana's claims against the 3 defendants, and then Edward's claims, finally deciding whether or not the two plaintiffs should bring one or two actions.

A. Diana's claims:

Generally speaking, with differences to be discussed under the section devoted to each defendant, Diana's claim is directed toward product liability. The general principles involved in this subject have evolved from the operation of both tort and contract principles. Some of the principles involved in such a mixture of tort and contract are conflicting: it is therefore necessary that some principles must yield to others. We will therefore examine the policy reasons behind the various rules, the conflicting principles, and the general trend of the law.

Under the common law, there was no contract liability without privity. This was based on policy decisions not to make a promisor or offeror an insurer of the world at large, and stemmed from a horror of contract liability to unknown and unforeseen plaintiffs, a principle also involved in tort law. In the earliest cases against manufacturers of products only the party who contracted *directly* with the manufacturer was allowed to recover for the latter's negligence. At first, this was a reasonable rule, where buyers generally contracted *directly* with the manufacturer who often built a coach or other product specifically to meet his customer's needs. On this basis, the manufacturer could *only* be held liable to his cus-

tomer for a breach of contract and perhaps
for negligence in tort.

As industry began to develop, however,
the requirement of *privity* became imprac-
tical where the buyer was frequently not the
final purchaser or consumer. Accordingly,
the rules of law began to change slowly.
First, the requirement of *privity* of contract
was rejected by J. Cardozo in *MacPherson,*
where the defendant auto manufacturer was
held liable for defects in an auto to the ultimate consumer, although a dealer had in-
tervened between manufacturer and the sale
to plaintiff. In that case, the requirement
of *negligence* continued to be stressed, although the auto company had *not* manufactured the defective wheel which caused
plaintiff's injuries. The court held that the
burden of care correlates with the probability of injury from a defective product,
and that here, where an auto was *known*
to be a dangerous instrument, the defendant
had a duty of *inspection* which would have
revealed the defective wheel and which duty
the defendant had breached. All of the elements of negligence were present in *Mac-
Pherson* and the court's holding was, primarily, that an assembler of autos is under
a duty of care to the ultimate user and will

be held liable for his *negligence,* his lack
of reasonable care under the particular circumstances, to the user of the auto where
the user could *not* be expected to inspect or
discover defects in the exercise of reasonable
care. This was true even though the manu-
facturer-assembler had no *privity* with plaintiff.

Then in *Henningson* the manufacturer of
a dangerously defective auto was held *strictly* liable *without* negligence to an injured
user. The court found that public policy
requires such liability of the manufacturer,
suggesting that the risk of harm must be
placed on the party best able to assume the
burden, and indicating that where a party
buys or uses a product placed on the market
for that use, there is an implied warranty of
its *fitness* for that use, running to him and
that express disclaimers of liability are void
as a matter of public policy.

All courts follow *MacPherson,* although
fewer courts have extended the *Henningson*
doctrine of strict liability without negligence.

The essential policy arguments involve
compensation of the innocent, injured party
—a general tort principle, placing the risk of

[214]

loss upon the party best able to bear and
distribute the burden, and imposing a duty
of care to others—another general tort principle.

a) Archer Ltd.—the manufacturer of the
gear transmission. Archer advertised in a
national magazine that its transmission
would never fail. If Father had expressly
relied upon the advertisement, there would
be a problem of *express* warranty liability
here. However, absent these facts it is unnecessary to linger upon the problem of
whether an advertisement directed to the
public-at-large reasonably constitutes an express warranty. It probably does not.

An *implied* warranty by Archer is all that
is required here, or in most any other products-liability case. The implied warranty is
that a product, placed upon the market and
intended for use by those who cannot reasonably be expected to inspect or to discover
any defects in that product, is reasonably
fit for the purpose for which it was intended.
To argue for Diana against Archer it should
be argued that Archer's transmission was
intended to 1) be assembled into bicycles
by others, 2) that such others could reasonably be expected to accept it as manufac-

tured, except for *obvious* defects, without
extensive inspection, 3) that such transmission was *intended* to be used by riders of
bicycles, and 4) that Archer warranted that
it was *reasonably fit* for such use. It will
be difficult to *prove* negligence against
Archer, for Diana cannot prove that the
transmission was in no way changed, damaged, or tampered with after leaving their
hands. Therefore, the best argument
against them is one of *strict liability*. However, as the court may *reject* that argument,
it must also be argued that the accident involving the gear transmission *infers* a breach
of their duty to exercise the care incident to
the probable risk of injury from a defective
bike transmission, which in the exercise of
reasonable care in manufacturing should
have worked properly as a *new* bicycle. All
of these allegations were either *expressly*
stated or implied in the advertisement
which, although probably *not* an express
warranty, is presumptive evidence of the
defendant's knowledge of its *own* duty to
exercise the reasonable care commensurate
with the nature and intended use of the product. This argument is *very* close to *res ipsa
loquitur*. However, since Diana is unable
to show that the instrumentality of injury

(here the transmission of the bike, specifically) was in the exclusive control of defendant,
Archer, and had *not* been tampered with
from the time it left Archer until her Father
purchased it, the negligence argument will
probably be rejected.

The *only* basis for Archer's liability, then,
that is likely to be accepted by the court is
that of strict liability, which will not necessarily be accepted everywhere.

b) Byke Co.—The same general arguments for product liability—either strict liability without negligence or liability for negligence—without privity, apply here. Byke
Co. is arguably in the position of a component manufacturer like Archer since it did
not assemble the bikes, but did manufacture
them and attached the gear transmission to
the rear wheel assembly in preparation for
shipment to Byke *dealers* who would assemble them according to Byke's specifications. While Byke *is* arguably a manufacturer of *component* parts, it nevertheless
was responsible for the *entire* bicycle, disas-
sembled, but complete. It is *more* difficult
to attribute *negligence* for the defective gear
transmission to Byke without proof that
they in fact *caused* the defect. If Byke

shipped *assembled* bikes it would be easier to impose liability as for the defective wheel in *MacPherson*. Arguably, it can be said that Byke had a *duty* to inspect the gear transmission for any defects as a *likely* instrumentality of harm in its bikes, and that selling them under its own name, with "built by Byke Co." visible on *even* the models where Coast-to-Coast replaced the brand name with its *own* name, imposes a duty to exercise the care commensurate with the hazard, which it has failed to exercise. The negligence argument for Byke's liability is stronger than it was for Archer, although still geared to the *fitness* of product argument which is equally applicable for negligence and strict liability.

Again, strict liability *must* be argued, that Byke impliedly warrants reasonable *fitness* of its bicycles when assembled according to their specifications and that in the *absence* of evidence of negligence by Coast-to-Coast, the burden should fall upon Byke to *disprove* its liability by showing that Coast was *negligent* in mis-assembling Diana's bike.

Because of Byke's contract with Coast-to-Coast, whereby the former disclaims all liability for warranty by contract, a new problem arises.   However, I believe that Byke could *still* be held liable *either* under a negligence or strict liability theory, *despite* the waiver of warranty.   This argument is based upon the *Henningson* case but is broader in its scope than liability without fault, the concept of such disclaimers being *void* as a matter of public policy.   No court retains the requirement of *privity,* and the ultimate user should therefore *not* be bound by the contractual obligations of other parties with respect to the product.   Therefore, in the absence of proof of Coast-to-Coast's *negligence,* Byke should be held liable on either a negligence or strict liability theory based on *fitness* of the product (strict liability, essentially) and a duty of care to *inspect* commensurate with the hazard (negligence).   Few courts (if any) have been willing to impose strict liability on the manufacturer of the *component* part (i. e. Archer) although virtually all courts hold the *manufacturer* liable for the product as a whole, even where the product has changed hands and there may have been a duty on the commercial dealer or user to inspect it in the exercise of reasonable care as well.   I point here to the *Kohlman-Lockheed-Am. Airlines* case, where Lockheed was held liable for the defective altimeter built by Kohlman, *even though* the plane was in the *exclusive* control of American Airlines who had a *duty* to inspect it regularly, and keep it in good repair. Lockheed's liability may have been based upon distribution of the risk, placing the *burden* of compensating loss on a party not only capable of absorbing that burden, but also responsible for manufacturing the airplane as a *whole*. The same policies apply to the instant case, where it may be *too great* a burden to impose liability upon Archer when the transmission has changed hands several times, and where Byke is really *responsible* for the product in the absence of evidence of Coast-to-Coast's negligence in assembling the bicycle.

The *Lockheed* case *does* suggest that in the future some courts may impose strict liability upon the *component* manufacturer although it isn't essential here, where the primary aim is simply to *compensate* Diana and Edward.

c) Coast-to-Coast—this is the basis of Edward's claim and also one of the defendants joined by Diana. Coast-to-Coast is most likely liable under both a negligence *and* strict liability theory, *if* the court finds in regard to strict liability that Coast-to-Coast had *sufficient* control over the product and sufficient responsibility for its fitness to warrant the imposition of strict liability, a doubtful finding. In general, retailers have been held liable to their customers (privity here) for *any* kind of express warranty and for *implied* warranty of its fitness long before the manufacturer was held liable despite a *lack* of privity. For both children, neither of whom was in direct *privity* with Coastar, warranty liability depends upon Coast-to-Coast's statement to the father that it would be "in full working order", "fully assembled" and "ready to go". This may *not* be an *express* warranty as it was an oral statement but it *certainly* is an *implied* warranty and the words were reasonably *intended* for father to *rely* upon them. This, together with its contractual obligation with Byke to assume all liability against Coastar should be sufficient to impose liability under *either* a theory of negligence and failure to exercise reasonable care to inspect where the *duty* was commensurate with the *probable* harm to be expected from defects in the instrumentality, or under a theory of *strict* liability or implied warranty of fitness, which here was made *explicitly* to Father.

[*221*]

I have no doubt but that Edward will be able to recover *something* from Coast-to-Coast, but if separate actions were brought, Diana's tried first and the three defendants, or Byke and Coast-to-Coast, were held *jointly* liable or with damages *apportioned* among them, the degree of Coast-to-Coast's liability may be *res judicata,* in which case Edward well may not be fully compensated. It is therefore more desirable for Diana and Edward to *join* their actions and for Edward to join Byke and Archer as defendants in his action against Coast-to-Coast. In that way, neither Diana *nor* Edward would be endangered by *res judicata.*

I have not dwelt here on proximate cause or causation-in-fact. Causation-in-fact is quite obvious. As for *proximate* cause, the plaintiffs are certainly *foreseeable* plaintiffs, for it is *expected* that bicycles will be used by *minors* who will not be expected to carefully *inspect* them, and the gear transmission defect was obviously the *proximate* cause of their injuries without efficient intervening cause. It could be argued that Edward was *not* a foreseeable plaintiff, but when Diana fell, the fall *proximately* and *partially* caused by the defective transmission, it should reasonably be foreseen that she might injure another bicyclist in her fall. It is reasonably foreseeable that young people and children will utilize a bicycle, and the *privity* argument has virtually dropped out of the vocabulary for products liability anyway.

.   .   .   .   .   .

COMMENT: This answer is well-written and covers about as many issues, with about as good analysis and penetration, as could be expected under the time limitations and conditions of an exam.

.   .   .   .   .   .

MARGINAL ANSWER

I

Diana against Archer, Byke Co. and Coast-to-Coast involves varied issues, most of which are in the area of products-liability. In Diana's action against Archer, it is first significant to note the Life advertisement telling of the quality of Archer gears. It is significant in that the ad says, indirectly, that a shift from high to low gear can occur while going "over hill and dale". Since Diana was going downhill at the time of the accident, she certainly seems to have been using the bicycle not only for its generally intended purpose, but for the purpose contemplated by the ad as well. In rejoinder, Archer might assert several positions.

First, Archer could deny that the ad was in any way a warranty of the gear. Archer would say that the ad as a whole was nothing more than an offer and that their assertion that their product was the finest in the world was nothing more than the type of statement which appears on all products. Furthermore, Archer would argue that even if the ad were construed as a warranty, it was clearly directed at the bicycle manufacturer and assembler, and that there was no privity of contract between Archer and Diana. In evaluation, it is very unlikely that the ad would be construed as an express warranty to anybody. However, there is a basis for finding an *implied* warranty whether the ad existed or not. Diana would say that the function of the gears was to make bicycles operative and that this means the product is really directed to the ultimate consumer. She would argue that it cannot be expected that either Byke Co. or Coast-to-Coast would disassemble the gear due to its complex nature; also that the latters' roles were essentially those of packagers and retailers. Furthermore, the fact that the gear did not become defective for a period of time suggests that Byke and Coastar couldn't have detected the problem anyway. In reply Archer could claim that the gear was negligently *assembled* by Byke Co., but there is no evidence to support such an assertion.

Next, Archer might claim that Diana and Edward were either contributorily negligent or were guilty of aggravated negligence. Concerning aggravated negligence, while the conduct was clearly wilful there is no real evidence that it was negligent. If you can't race or speed a bike on a country road (assume it had packed gravel) there is no place for it to move swiftly. Besides, the race factor is not crucial in that the Byke was advertised as going up and down hill and going down hill will naturally cause a higher speed. The claim of contributory negligence rests on the alleged misuse of the gears in shifting into low gear while speeding down a hill which is clearly not a desirable practice. This is especially significant since Diana's father had no way of knowing (from the facts) that the gear was an Archer gear, which purported to allow the unusual shift-ing—thus avoiding a possible misrepresenta-tion issue. Rather, there is no evidence he saw the tiny Archer symbol, knew what it meant, or relied on it. However, thinking along *MacPherson* lines, the fact that the gears could give way which would lead to probable injury of some kind is foreseeable and probable. Diana would appear to have a good case against Archer.

Against Byke Co. Diana could argue that they had a duty not to put defective parts in their bicycle crates. However, the very na-ture of the defect, suggests that it probably wouldn't have been discovered by anything less than completely taking the gear apart which goes beyond the reasonableness of precaution burden of Byke Co. Further-more, Byke company had waived its war-ranties under contract with Coast-to-Coast.

Diana's action against Coast-to-Coast will probably not succeed. The mere assembly of the bike has not made an incredibly dif-ferent product in that the gear was clearly designed for bicycle use. Furthermore, put-ting a different name on the bicycle, didn't remake or remold the product. Also since Coast-to-Coast was only an assembler and retailer, it couldn't have a duty other than to discover the most obvious defects.

Edward's claim against Coast-to-Coast will not stand up due to his remoteness to the transaction. He cannot be perceived as an ultimate consumer and clearly he is not in privity with anyone.

.   .   .   .   .   .

COMMENT: This answer is fairly well written and organized, as far as it goes, but a comparison with the "A" answer shows how many of the possible issues are not dealt with at all here. In particular, this answer does not really explore at all the very important questions of the various bases of product-liability—i. e., negligence, strict liability and warranty, the problems of privity, etc. It is thus quite superficial and of marginal adequacy at best. Furthermore, some of the statements as to the facts and law are inaccurate.

TORTS (III)

(one and one-quarter hours)

Boney Skelton owned a wild and desolate piece of land at the corner of Skull Road and Pixie Lane. On the property was an old abandoned farm house in an advanced state of decay. For fifty years, since Boney's uncle, Cad Aver, was found hanging from a rafter in the attic with his wife Cattabuke's body still smoldering in the fireplace, the house had been known in the community as "The Haunted House." The neighbors often reported strange noises coming from the house, lights flashing at night, and on moonlight nights red eyes peering from the windows. Several months before the events in question a deathly stench which attracted buzzards was traced to the house. Boney Skelton investigated and found in the basement the remains of an unidentified man. He apparently was a tramp who had taken refuge in the house during a storm, fallen through a trap door into the basement and was killed. Boney replaced the door and also carefully investigated the house. He saw evidence that the house had frequently been used by tramps, that squirrels and various birds had taken up residence in the attic and other animals had occupied the basement. Many of the floors were badly rotted and the stairs were near collapse.

The Haunted House was a perennial subject of conversation among boys in the neighborhood, who frequently went to explore, but most often returned without doing more than looking in the windows. A few of the most adventurous did enter but were unable to prove or disprove the presence of ghosts. Percy Philpot, a boy of twelve, was one of those who had often declared he was not afraid, but had never gotten closer than the front gate which hung precariously from one hinge. Percy's father, Erwin, purchased from a friend a Great Dane watchdog named Dracula, a veteran of the K–9 Corps. Erwin was told that the dog was trained to protect both the property and members of the family from any threat of harm. It had frequently chased off intruders but had never bitten anyone.

Several weeks after Dracula was obtained, Percy took it with him to explore the Haunted House. With the dog by his side, Percy entered the house. He looked into several downstairs rooms and then started up the stairs. When he got to the landing half-way up the stairs he heard a loud moan, the rattling of chains, the stamping of feet and then a door slammed. Frightened out of his wits, Percy gave a blood-curdling scream, fainted, and fell against the stair rail which collapsed and catapulted him to the floor below. Dracula charged up the stairs where he found Wun Lei Low, a fugitive from justice who had been using the house as a hideout for over a month. Low had heard Percy enter the house and had made the noises in hopes of encouraging Percy to leave and not return. Dracula rushed at Low who tried to fend him off with a chair. Finally he sought to escape the dog by jumping out a front window.

In the meantime, German Colt, a hunter, was approaching the house from the rear. He heard Percy's scream, Dracula's barking and Low's shouting. He rushed into the house through the back door only to fall through the trap door mentioned above. He fell into the basement and was disabled. Colt had earlier approached Boney about hunting on this land. Boney had agreed that Colt could hunt there so long as he would give Boney one-half of the game. In the course of their conversation Boney had mentioned how various animals had not seemed deterred by the reputation of the house.

Dracula's barking attracted a passerby who found the three injured persons. Percy's arm was broken in the fall. Low suffered a minor bite on his left leg, inflicted by Dracula, and a broken right leg from the fall. Colt suffered a broken back and was permanently disabled.

    (a) Percy sues Skelton

    (b) Percy sues Low

    (c) Low sues Erwin Philpot

    (d) Colt sues Skelton

    (e) Colt sues Low

Write a memorandum in which you evaluate the likelihood of recovery in each of the above mentioned suits, setting forth the bases for your evaluation.

. . . . . .

ANSWERS TO TORTS (III)
GOOD "A" ANSWER

(A) *Percy v. Skelton*

Percy would sue Skelton for negligent infliction of harm. (Percy would not have a cause of action against Skelton for intentional infliction of harm because Skelton did not act either for the purpose of harming Percy or with knowledge that to a substantial certain-

ty Percy would be harmed.)   The essential
elements of a cause of action for negligence
are:

1) that the defendant owed a duty of care
to the plaintiff;

2) that the defendant breached that duty
by violating a standard of conduct established
by law for protection of plaintiff;

3) that the defendant's negligence (i. e.
breach of duty) was both a factual and proximate cause of the plaintiff's injury; and

4) that the injury suffered by plaintiff is
recognized by law as compensable.

The duty of care owed by a landowner to
an entrant upon the land depends upon the
classification of the entrant. Percy was clearly a trespasser, since he entered Skelton's
land without the express or implied consent
of Skelton and not pursuant to any other
recognized privilege.   Ordinarily, the only
duty owed by a landowner to a trespasser is
not to set traps for the trespasser. If the
landowner knows of the presence of the trespasser, he has the duty to use reasonable care
with respect to active operations on the land
and to warn such discovered trespasser of
hidden dangers, if such warning is feasible
under the circumstances. In most jurisdic-

tions, if a landowner knows, or has reason to know, that persons frequently trespass on limited areas of his land, he has the same duty with respect to those persons as he has with respect to a discovered trespasser—that is, he must conduct operations on the land so as not to create an unreasonable risk of harm and he must either remedy or adequately warn of dangerous conditions. It seems clear that Skelton owed such duty to Percy. Skelton's investigation of the house several months before Percy's accident disclosed that the house was frequented by trespassers. In addition, it seemed to be general knowledge in the community that a variety of persons entered the land and house.

Since Skelton knew, or at the very least had reason to know, that trespassers frequently went on the land and into the house, he was under a duty either to keep the house in proper repair or adequately warn of the dangers. Since he did neither, Percy should have no difficulty establishing that Skelton breached the duty of care which he owed Percy.

There is a second basis on which Percy could establish that Skelton owed a duty of care to Percy—the "attractive nuisance" doc-

trine. Most jurisdictions hold that a landowner owes a duty of ordinary care with
respect to trespassing children if 1) he main-
tains an artificial condition on his land, 2)
the condition is dangerous to children, 3)
children are likely to be exposed to it, and 4)
the children are not likely to appreciate the
nature or extent of the danger. It seems that
all of the essential elements for application of
the attractive nuisance doctrine exist in this
case. Percy might have some difficulty establishing that children of his age could not
be expected to appreciate the nature and extent of the danger involved. But my guess is
that he will be able to do so.

Percy will have no difficulty establishing
that Skelton's breach of duty was a cause in
fact of Percy's injury. It is not necessary
that the defendant's breach of duty be the
sole cause in fact of the plaintiff's injury. It
is sufficient if the defendant's breach of duty
is *a* cause in fact. A breach of duty is a
cause in fact of injury if the injury would not
have occurred but for the breach of duty (the
so-called *"sine qua non"* test). That was
clearly the case here. If Percy had adequately maintained the railings in the house, or
if he had adequately warned of the dangers,

Percy would not have been injured—or at least a jury could so find.

Finally, Percy should be able to establish at least a jury question with respect to proximate cause. There are two primary tests for proximate cause. One is the "direct results" or "Polemis" test and the other is the "risk principle" or "Wagon Mound" test. In this particular case, Percy should get to the jury under either one. The "direct result" test provides that a given act (or failure to act) is the proximate cause of a given injury if the injury proceeded directly from the act without any intervening, superseding cause, Skelton might argue that the act of Low was an intervening, superseding cause. But for an intervening cause to be superseding it must not be reasonably foreseeable. Under the circumstances, it was certainly foreseeable that a tramp might be in the house and that he might cause harm to a trespassing child. The "Wagon-Mound" test provides that a given act is the proximate cause of a given injury if the injury was a reasonably foreseeable consequence of the act. It is not required that the particular details of the injury or its manner of occurrence be foreseeable—only the general type of injury. Percy should be able to show that the general type of injury he suffered was a reasonably foreseeable consequence of Skelton's breach of duty.

Skelton will no doubt allege that Percy was contributorily negligent and that Percy assumed the risk of injury. Contributory negligence is lack of due care by a plaintiff which contributes causally to his injuries. The standard by which contributory negligence of a child is measured is: what precaution would be adopted by a child of the same age, intelligence and experience. I doubt that Skelton will be able to establish this defense because Percy was only twelve years old, and a jury is likely to conclude that he was behaving as carefully as the average 12-year-old would under the circumstances.

Assumption of risk applies when the plaintiff expressly assumes the risk or when he impliedly assumes it. He impliedly assumes the risk when he understands the nature and extent of the risk and deliberately exposes himself to it. It is clear that there was no express assumption of risk in this case. And in my opinion, in view of the age of Percy, it is unlikely that Skelton will be able to prove that Percy appreciated the nature and extent of the risk to which Percy exposed himself.

(B) *Percy v. Low*

There are three theories on which Percy might sue Low: battery, assault and intentional infliction of mental distress.

Battery is the intended infliction of a harmful or offensive bodily contact. The requisite intent exists when the plaintiff proves either that the defendant acted for the purpose of causing the contact or with knowledge that to a substantial certainty the contact would follow. It is not necessary that the contact with the plaintiff's body be made by the defendant or something under defendant's control. It is sufficient, if, for example, the defendant intentionally causes the plaintiff to fall.

On the facts of this case, Percy will have no trouble proving bodily contact (he fell through the railing and to the floor) or causally-related injury. He also will have no trouble proving that Low acted intentionally. But he may have difficulty proving that Low intended to cause bodily contact. There does not seem to be sufficient evidence to support purposive intent. It is a close question as to whether the court would permit a jury to infer that Low knew to a substantial certainty that Percy would fall. I think not. Low acted for the purpose of frightening Percy into leaving the premises. Causing Percy to fall seems inconsistent with that purpose. So, Percy is unlikely to prevail in a cause of action for battery.

The second theory on which Percy might base his suit against Low is assault. Assault is the intentional creation of anticipation of a harmful or offensive bodily contact. If actual bodily contact ensues, any resulting injury is recoverable as a form of parasitic damages. Again the intent which is an essential element of this tort can be either purposive intent or substantial certainty intent. Since it was obviously Low's purpose to make young Percy think there were ghosts in the house and consequently to flee the premises, Percy may have difficulty proving that Low acted either for the purpose of putting Percy in fear of imminent bodily contact or with knowledge that to a substantial certainty Percy would fear imminent bodily contact. This is a close question, but since the fear of bodily contact must be reasonable under the circumstances my guess is that Percy is not likely to prevail in a cause of action for assault.

The final theory on which Percy might base his suit against Low is intentional infliction of severe mental distress. The essential elements of this tort are conduct by the defendant accompanied by the intent (purposive or substantial certainty) to inflict severe mental distress and the resulting distress. The mental distress suffered by the plaintiff must be reasonable under the circumstances, but the court will take into consideration any unusual susceptibility of the plaintiff to distress which the defendant should know of. Resulting physical injury is compensable as a form of parasitic damages. I think Percy has a good chance of prevailing on this theory. On the facts, it is clear that Low acted for the purpose of frightening Percy. In fact he wanted to frighten Percy to the extent that Percy would flee. In addition, Low could reasonably be expected to appreciate Percy's unusual susceptibility to distress because of his age and the circumstances. Percy can prove resulting distress and bodily injury directly resulting from the distress.

(C) *Low v. Erwin Philpot*

The theory of Low's suit against Philpot would be strict liability for the keeping of an animal with known dangerous propensities. The dog was trained as a watch dog by the army; Philpot had been informed that it would protect the family members and property from harm; and the animal had chased persons on prior occasions. Under these circumstances, a court is likely to conclude— or at least allow a jury to conclude—that Philpot knew the animal had vicious propensities.

Philpot might defend the suit on two grounds (in addition to any assertion that he did not know of the animal's vicious propensities): First, the scope of strict liability for keeping a vicious animal is limited to harm which is reasonably foreseeable as a consequence of the viciousness. Philpot might argue that the reasonably foreseeable risk of harm was dog bite, and here Low was injured from a fall. I doubt that Philpot would prevail with such a defense, because the animal was trained to chase and had chased others in the past. One of the foreseeable risks of harm would be that a person running from the dog would fall and be injured. My guess is that a court would so conclude. Second, Philpot might defend on the ground that Low had assumed the risk by deliberately "antagonizing" the animal with his wild noises and his attempt to frighten Percy. Although contributory negligence is not ordinarily a

defense to strict liability, assumption of risk
in the sense of deliberate exposure of oneself
to a known risk of harm is. It is true that
Low did not know the dog was trained as
part of the K–9 Corps, but a court would
probably conclude—or let a jury conclude—
that Low appreciated that any animal might
attack in these circumstances. My guess is
that a court would so conclude. (It would be
inclined to do so because of Low's outlaw
status). And therefore Low is not likely to
win his suit against Philpot.

(D) *Colt v. Skelton*

Colt's suit against Skelton would be for
negligence. Colt was a business invitee on
Skelton's land. He was there pursuant to
Skelton's express permission and for a purpose which involved a pecuniary benefit to
Skelton (one half of game shot by Colt). A
landowner owes a business invitee the duty
of exercising reasonable care under the circumstances. Colt had not exercised reasonable care by maintenance of the trap door
through which Colt fell.

Skelton might defend on the ground that
Colt was not a business invitee with respect
to the house. He was only given permission
to hunt on the land. Therefore, Colt was a

trespasser in the house and Skelton's only
duty was to warn Colt of danger and such
warning was not feasible under the circumstances. Colt could argue that the permission to enter Skelton's land extended to the
house since permission was granted for the
purpose of hunting and Skelton had expressly
mentioned that animals were in the house.
In addition Colt might argue that Skelton
owed him a duty of ordinary care even if
permission did not extend to use of the house,
because Skelton knew the house was frequented by trespassers. (This basis of duty
is discussed above in connection with Percy's
suit against Skelton.)

(E) *Colt v. Low*

Colt's suit against Low would probably
have to be for negligent infliction of injury,
since Low did not know of Colt's presence,
and therefore did not act for the purpose of
injuring Colt or with knowledge to a substantial certainty that Colt would be injured.
Low might argue that Colt cannot recover
for negligence because neither his presence
nor his injury was reasonably foreseeable as
a consequence of Low's action. Colt might
respond by arguing the rescue doctrine—
that is, he might argue that under the cir-

cumstances it was reasonable to expect that someone would hear Percy and attempt to come to his rescue. My guess is that the court would agree with Colt and that he will win in the suit against Low for negligence.

Colt may also base his suit against Low on assault and on battery. The essential elements of those causes of action have been set forth above in my discussion of Percy's suit against Low. There is a general principle that where the requisite intent for assault or battery exists and some one other than the intended victim is injured the intent may be "transferred" to the injured third party, allowing him to recover in assault or battery for his injury. That principle should apply here. The difficulty, as discussed above, will be the requisite intent vis a vis Percy, so that such intent could be "transferred" to Colt.

.   .   .   .   .   .

COMMENT: Some students who analyze quickly and write rapidly are able to write long, detailed answers, like this one in the allotted time. Others are not able to write this much. However, the quality of the answer and the grade it will receive do not depend on the number of words written. They depend upon how many of the relevant issues

are dealt with and how well the facts are analyzed in light of the applicable law and the soundness of the reasoning in reaching conclusions on the issues. Thus, a substantially shorter, more concise answer to this problem could receive as good a grade as this one if it covered the same points adequately.

.   .   .   .   .

MARGINAL ANSWER

The five following lawsuits, are to be determined primarily by ascertaining (1) what was the standard of care (SC) due plaintiff by defendant; (2) did defendant violate that standard, and (3) were there any damages pursuant to that breach?

(A) Percy sues Skelton.

In this action, it is vital to determine whether Percy was an invitee or a trespasser, for there is a different standard of care owed to each one by Skelton.

The argument could be raised by Percy, that it was common knowledge that people went to the House, and that Skelton had never forbade Percy from going onto Skelton's property. It could also be alleged, that the House was paradoxically attractive to boys because of its forboding atmosphere.

Yet the mere absence of dissent is not to be interpreted as consent. If A walks away with B's television set, he has no defense in saying that B had never told him *not* to take the television. Then if permission or a lack of a denial of permission is not the gist of the question, one can find that the difference between a trespasser and an invitee, is the actual words or actions which give the actor the owner's consent. Such consent is missing here. If the allegation is sustained that defendant's lack of putting up signs is an indication that he did not care if people visited his property, then why can't the theory be advanced that the fence around the property was an outward manifestation that Skelton wanted no visitors. Since both the theories are, on the main, groundless they both should be dismissed, leaving the plaintiff as a person who entered Skelton's property without permission, and therefore with the characteristics of a trespasser.

The duty owed to a trespasser is only that the owner does not commit any intentional torts upon the trespasser. It does not matter if the owner knows who the trespasser is, in order for the owner to be liable. If he sets a trap or spring-gun against trespassers as a class, then he is liable to any individual trespasser. It may be argued that Skelton was negligent in not keeping his house in good repair, but this will not advance the plaintiff's case.

Yet, even if the court were to deem Percy an invitee because of the prevailing local custom, there is still a bar to his recovery.

A handrail is arguably an instrument which has as a main purpose to steady the stair climber rather than support him as he falls against it. A handrail can be an effective guide, without being strong enough to support a person. It is therefore arguable that Skelton was not negligent in maintaining the handrail in a state of repair permitting it to be used for what it was designed. It also can be affirmatively alleged by Skelton that by entering the house Percy (1) was contributorily negligent and (2) did assume the risk which a normal person 12 years old would appreciate to be connected with "an old abandoned farm house in an advanced state of decay," which was so far gone that the front gate "hung precariously from one hinge." A reasonable child that age could have anticipated the dangers.

It is very doubtful that Percy can obtain judgment.

(B) Percy can conceivably sue Low for both (1) mental distress and (2) assault.

Mental distress, because of its difficulty in asserting monetary damages, is sometimes hard to build a sound case upon. However, Minnesota has awarded damages for pure mental distress, as in Johnson v. Sampson where school officials accused a girl of being unchaste. It is much easier to build a case if the plaintiff has also suffered physical damage because of the mental distress. It is certainly obvious that Low intended to disturb Percy by scaring him, and it is also true that the boy's broken arm was a result of that fall.

The assault in this case was the deliberately raising of apprehension of a battery. There is no unintentional assault, and the main reason for Low committing the aforementioned tort, of mental distress, was to make Percy feel that he was in immediate danger of being the victim of a battery. No damages need be proven in an assault case. The court has found defendants liable for assault when the acts were done as a practical joke or when the defendant thought the action was for the plaintiff's own good. Percy should recover.

(C) Low would be suing on some kind of a vicarious liability theory, that Erwin was re-

sponsible for the actions of his unemancipated son Percy. Quite often in these cases,
the capacity to sue brings with it the capacity
to be sued. There is a strong possibility that
if someone inflicts a tort on an unemancipated child, the parent can sue as guardian.
Yet so can someone who has been given the
unemancipated child's rights, such as an out-
of-state representative who is brought in for
jurisdictional reasons. Can he too, be sued
on the child's behalf for any tort the child
may have committed upon another?

State v. Cateetes, to a large degree, answers the preceding questions. Yet the present controversy can be decided on other
grounds.

Dracula, like Erwin's car, is owned by Erwin. He is responsible for his car's and his
dog's actions. If Percy was driving the car
and he struck Low, then Low could sue Erwin. Then what is the standard of care which
is expected of Dracula, a breach of the standard which would rain down liability upon Erwin? What are Erwin's obligations?

One must consider Dracula's massive size
and training. Although he is gifted with a
great deal of strength, he was also orientated
to be a watchdog. This, then puts him into

another category, away from the average household pet group. His owner must exercise more care in seeing that third persons are not injured. He either was negligent in keeping Dracula in a place where Percy could get him or else he let Percy take the dog, thereby assuming responsibilities.

Even though Low did commit a tort on Percy, the action was over when the dog started to confront Low. If the dog had tried to save Percy from a tort an argument might be made that there was self-defense involved.

If the jury can find that Low acted as a reasonable man would act under the circumstances i. e. jumping out a window to escape an enraged dog, then Low can recover for his injuries.

(D) Since Colt had a right to enter Skelton's premises because of the contract with Skelton that Colt would give him ½ of his catch, Colt can be put into the class of business invitee. Colt attempted to enter the building knowing that Skelton had told him that there were animals inside. Still, Colt did enter with his main purpose, apparently, to investigate the commotion. Yet he was near the house, perhaps with the intention of entering.

Skelton was under an obligation to tell Colt of any defects which might injure Colt. And even if the assertion could be sustained that Colt did not enter with the intention to hunt, it still would have to be proven by Skelton, as an affirmative defense, that this relieved him from liability. Yet there is the other factor that Skelton replaced a faulty trap door, which action might not help a trespasser to secure a judgment, is damning to his attempt to avoid liability to an invitee. Colt had permission to enter Skelton's house, Skelton knew of the danger yet did not warn Colt (even though another man had been killed) and he is therefore liable for his negligence.

(E) Colt can get nothing from Low. Any of Low's action can't be deemed to have put Colt in danger, either through direct intent or even the slightest negligence.

At the time Colt arrived, Low wasn't even in the house. He was on the front lawn with a broken leg, as Colt went in the back door.

Colt entered out of curiosity and he had no duty to enter. He acted and was entering the house (1) because he had permission from Skelton and (2) because he wanted to.

PROPERTY (I)

(one hour)

Adam owned Blackacre in fee simple absolute. He died on January 1, 1968 leaving a duly executed will which, in the portion relevant to this question, provided:

> "To my beloved son Bede and his heirs I give, bequeath and devise Blackacre and all my other real property but if my son Bede dies without issue, then it is my will that Blackacre go to my son Carl or his heirs."

Shortly after the death of Adam, Bede duly executed and delivered a deed to Dave which described Blackacre and purported to convey the land "to Dave and his heirs."

Bede died on January 1, 1971, survived by Carl. Bede had never married and his duly executed will left everything that he owned to his friend, Eva.

Write an opinion on the state of the title to Blackacre. Assume that the developed common law of Real Property is in force including English statutes passed up to 1700.

．   ．   ．   ．   ．   ．

COMMENT: Examination problem-questions in Real Property, and to some extent in Personal Property, normally involve primarily an analysis and determination of the types of estates or other property interests created in various parties by the particular conveyance(s) or other transfer(s) specified in the problem, the effect on such interests of specified subsequent acts and events, and the resultant state of the title to or ownership of the property involved and the rights, powers, privileges and immunities incident thereto. Thus, the answers will differ in material respects from those required for the normal Contracts or Torts problems where the primary concern is whether on the facts given the essentials exist for civil liability of one party to another for damage from breach of contract or tortious behavior and, if so, what remedies may be available. Both types of problems require recognition and analysis of the issues involved in light of applicable law and the facts, and the probable conclusions therefrom, but the nature and objectives of the analysis are different in the Property problems and this should be recognized in writing a Property exam.

For the purpose of grading the answers to a Real Property problem like the one above, the examiner, instead of preparing a detailed summary of possible issues and sub-issues, might write out a comprehensive analysis like the following to use as a standard for comparison and evaluation.

PROFESSOR'S ANALYSIS USED AS STANDARD FOR GRADING

Issues involved:

1. What is the meaning of the words "dies without issue."

2. What kind of interest or interests are created by the gift over to "Carl or his heirs."

3. What is the effect of the deed from Bede to Dave shortly after the death of Adam.

4. What is the effect on the title of the death of Bede in 1971.

1. What is the meaning of the words "dies without issue."

The will uses language which gives a fee simple to Bede and it might be argued that the words following the gift to Bede are merely precatory but the developed common law would give effect so far as possible to all of

[*253*]

the language used in the will so that the
meaning of the words "dies without issue"
must be determined. At one stage of develop-
ment these words would have created a fee
tail in Bede by construing them as meaning
indefinite failure of issue. Powell on Real
Property, Sec. 340. If this construction is
utilized then the interests created by the gift
over could not take effect until the line of
Bede's descendants became extinct; that is,
they would follow a fee tail, not cut short a
fee simple and their nature would be different. The later common law, however, would
construe these words as meaning definite failure of issue; that is, the gift over could take
effect only if the failure of issue occurred by
some definite date, such as the death of Bede
in this case.

2. What kind of interest or interests are
    created by the gift over to "Carl or his
    heirs."

The formal necessity of the word heirs was
relaxed in relation to testamentary disposi-
tions. Since it was clear from the testator's
language that Bede was to have an estate of
fee duration the gift over to Carl can be
found to manifest an intent that it be of fee
duration. Powell on Real Property Sec. 183.

Since the words "or his heirs" are used instead of the words "and his heirs" of the first gift it is possible that the word heirs is intended as a word of purchase rather than a word of limitation. If the indefinite failure of issue construction is adopted this would make the interests over remainders of a contingent alternative type or possibly the interest in Carl is a remainder for life with a contingent remainder over to the heirs of Carl. Such a construction sets up the possibility of the Rule in Shelley's case operating to create a fee interest in Carl. If the definite failure of issue construction is adopted then the interests over must be executory interests following a defeasible fee in Bede. If such is the construction then the Rule in Shelley's case is not applicable but the question would still exist whether the interest in Carl was of fee duration. The analysis above would lead to the finding under the developed common law of a fee in Carl contingent on Bede dying without issue and Carl surviving. There would be an alternative executory interest contingent on Carl's nonsurvival in the heirs of Carl. (It might be noted that the rule against perpetuities had no application to contingent remainders following a fee tail since the rule did not develop until fee tails had already become barrable, rendering them of no importance as fetters on alienation of land.)

3.   What is the effect of the deed from Bede to Dave shortly after the death of Adam.

The deed would convey to Dave whatever interests Bede had in Blackacre. It may be noted that the words "and all my other real property" in the will of Adam caused Bede to take any reversion that may have remained in the estate of Adam by virtue of the creation of a fee tail with contingent remainders. If the interests in Bede were a fee tail and a reversion by virtue of the will of Adam, then merger could occur in Dave which would destroy any contingent remainders in Carl and his heirs. Such destruction would not have occurred while these interests were in Bede since they were all created by the same instrument, the will of Adam. If, however, the interest in Bede is a fee simple defeasible then that is all that Dave got and the only significance of the conveyance is to remove Bede from the problem as an owner. It might be argued that the conveyance to Dave is a forfeiture by tortious conveyance if Bede has a fee tail; but since Bede has the reversion also, in this construction, the result seems to be the same, a fee simple in Dave, if the remainders are contingent. Such remainders would be destroyed by the forfeiture of their supporting estate. The idea of forfeiture by tortious conveyance may well have become formal and technical enough by 1700 to support this result. Note that if Carl's interest is a vested remainder, it would come to possessory status if the preceding estate is destroyed.

4. What is the effect on the title of the death of Bede in 1971.

Since Bede died without issue the interests in Carl and his heirs were qualified to take effect if not destroyed. Since they are not destroyed if they are not contingent remainders and since Carl survived Bede he took a fee simple unless his interest is construed as a life estate which is unlikely.

CONCLUSION

Assuming that the more modern construction of the will of Adam is adopted, the estate created in Bede is a fee subject to executory interests in Carl or his heirs. These interests are alternative executory interests in fee and are not destroyed by the doctrine of merger working in conjunction with the doctrine of destructibility of contingent remainders. The interest of Carl would thus vest in possession as a fee simple absolute. If, however, the older construction of indefinite failure of issue were used then the conveyance from Bede to Dave could have destroyed the contingent remainders following the fee tail and Dave would have the fee simple. Even if the modern construction of failure of issue is assumed there is one slight danger to the security of Carl's title. That is the possibility that the interest in Carl following the estate in Bede may be considered both an executory interest and for life. Under this rather remote construction there would be indestructible interests outstanding in the heirs of Carl who would not be ascertained until his death. Eva presents no legal problem since Bede had effectively divested himself of any interest by his conveyance to Dave prior to the time his will became effective.

.   .   .   .   .   .

ANSWERS TO PROPERTY (I)

GOOD "A" ANSWER

By the will of Adam he gave to Bede a fee simple determinable. That is, Bede has the land subject to a condition subsequent. That condition is that he die without issue. This could possibly be held to be a fee tail, and upon indefinite failure of issue a remainder over to Carl or his heirs. I would have to go along with a fee simple determinable, however, due to the operative words "to . . . Bede and his heirs." Heirs used in its technical sense.

What Carl has is not exactly clear. It is clear that if Bede has a determinable fee upon the condition of Bede dying without issue he has an executory interest. However, exactly what that executory interest is, I can't tell for sure. With the insertion of "or" in "to . . . Carl *or* his heirs" it looks like either Carl or his heirs could take. Now the only way the heirs could take would be (1) the court deems heirs not to be used in their technical sense: rather those children of Carl who are living at Bede's death. This would presumably be subject to divestment, i. e. more children could be born and reduce what those living children have. (2) The other way the heirs would take would be for Carl to also be dead. To cover this, Adam should have given a life estate to Carl with a remainder to his heirs, but this would have been defeated by the rule in Shelley's case.

If Adam knew anything about law he would have realized that to do this he must set up a trust. This is not what Adam did, however, so we are still stuck on knowing exactly what he intended. I believe what he wanted was for Carl to have a fee, but if Carl was dead at Bede's death without issue for the land to go to Carl's heirs. In view of the presumption that one cannot have heirs until dead this limitation of Carl's should be construed as a fee.

After Bede took by the death of Adam, he conveyed Blackacre to Dave and his heirs. This would assume that Bede had a fee simple to convey. This was not true. All he could give Dave was his determinable fee. If Bede died without children then the executory fee would arise, and Dave would have nothing.

As fate would have it for Dave, Bede did die without children, and was survived by Carl who now has the fee (assuming the problem of construction is settled in favor of a fee. In any event, Dave does not have title.) Bede purported to leave everything to Eva by will, but Eva can only take what Bede had. Blackacre was no longer his at his death, but she may have a claim on the rest of Adam's real property, because Carl's executory interest was only in Blackacre.

The only way Eva could claim Blackacre is by claiming that Bede had a fee tail, with a remainder over. At the death of Adam, Bede got his other real property interests, i. e. the reversion (if the remainder over was contingent, which it might be claimed that it is, as we are not sure what and how Carl or his heirs take; but this is not sound because Carl is ready to take and is an ascertained person in being, as would be his heirs if so designated, and the remainder would be vested) would go to Bede thereby merging the fee with the fee tail and destroying the contingent remainder (this implies that contingent remainders are still destructible by law. In Minnesota, for example, they are not and will vest upon the contingency being met.) This would mean that Bede had a fee simple, but this was conveyed to Dave, so as a matter of fact Eva can never have a claim on Blackacre, but Dave may. There is a possibility that upon Bede's death Carl is also dead and has no heirs. At this point Eva would get Blackacre. As it stands now, however, Carl takes a fee simple. But Eva could argue that Carl takes a life estate with nothing left for his heirs as the limitation is to Carl or heirs, which implies to the exclusion of the other. Then the will would read, in effect, "to my son, Carl," which can be either a life estate or a fee, depending on which jurisdiction you are in. If Eva can convince the court or if state statute says it is a life estate, Eva would have the reversion.

.   .   .   .   .   .

COMMENT: This answer presents a fairly well organized, concise analysis of most of the possible estates and interests created by the two wills and Bede's conveyance, and the effect thereon of the death of Bede without issue. It is not quite as well-written as it might be, but would still be considered a good "A" answer by most first-year instructors.

.   .   .   .   .   .

MARGINAL ANSWER

Adam by a duly executed will left to his son, Bede, a defeasible fee, subject to condition subsequent. The condition being that Bede must die leaving issue or the executory interest to Carl would rise up and divest Bede's fee.

Bede, before dying without issue, conveyed a deed in fee simple to Dave, this conveyance occurring after the death of Adam. Bede, however, could not convey a greater interest than he had himself. Dave could not take a full fee simple absolute, but took only the defeasible fee of Bede, and Bede's dying without issue invoked the condition and Carl took the complete fee in Blackacre destroying Dave's interest.

There is a problem as to what Bede had left to give to Eva after his death. The grant by Adam gave a fee, subject to defeasance, in Blackacre and in all other property.

Bede's conveyance to Dave of Blackacre, if not void because he conveyed more than he could, at least removed Blackacre from being given to Eva by will. Therefore the will leaving his remaining property to Eva does not affect Blackacre.

It therefore appears that the title to Blackacre has vested in Carl as an executory devisee.

But before coming to this conclusion we must trace the title along one more path. Adam's will may be construed to have given only a fee tail estate to Bede because it limited his fee to having issue. A fee tail today, in the majority of jurisdictions is given the effect of a life estate with contingent remain-

der to issue. If Bede's conveyance to Dave
could be considered void then we must consider Eva's interest. Eva was given all of
Bede's real and personal property. Bede
again could convey his vested interest in
Blackacre to Eva. The interest, however,
still carried the executory limitation, which
either came into effect or was itself defeated
at the death of Bede without issue. Bede did
die without ever having issue. Therefore at
his death any interest in Blackacre could not
be inherited by Eva, but shifted to Carl according to the Statute of Uses.

Dave and Eva may have a claim though,
but it will be a future interest in the land.
Adam's limitation to Carl may not have been
a fee, but a life estate. If so, then by the
doctrine of worthier title both sons, Bede and
Carl, would have a ½ interest in fee in Blackacre at the death of Adam. As this would
have occurred at the death of Adam, since
Bede conveyed only a fee interest to Dave
after the death of Adam, Dave may have
received a ½ interest in fee. This, of course,
would leave Eva nothing. But it would also
be likely that the deed as written could not
do this and would be void. Hence Eva,
through Bede's testamentary devise to her,

may possibly have a ½ interest in fee with Carl or the heirs of Carl.

The key problem therefore is the interpretation of the executory limitation, specifically the phrase: "to my son, Carl, or his heirs". This is not a technical way of giving a fee, the word "or" raises problems of construction. If it is construed to be a fee simple devise then Carl has all interest in Blackacre. However, if Carl received only a life estate, or his heirs (if determined at Adam's death), then through inheritance the grantees of the heirs of Bede may receive some interest.

.   .   .   .   .   .

COMMENT: This answer recognizes many of the issues and possible interests of the parties but is not well organized. Also, the reasoning and analysis is faulty on some points. The resultant confusion leaves the reader uncertain as to just what the writer's conclusions are as to the state of the title to Blackacre—the question asked in the problem—and makes it only marginally satisfactory at best.

PROPERTY (II)

(Closed-book except for Selected Statutes usable during exam)

(1 hour)

'Arry Abinger, an elderly retired lawyer who had been a constitutional law specialist in practice, was a lifelong resident of Sleepy Eye, Minnesota. He had much to be happy about as he lived out his declining years. He had accumulated a substantial estate; his son, Bing, and his daughter, Candy, had both married well and were prominent citizens of Sleepy Eye; and 'Arry, after being a widower for five years, had recently married Ursula, an attractive widow in town.

However, 'Arry was concerned about the high level of death taxes. Consequently, in an effort to reduce these taxes he decided to take the following steps:

(1) 'Arry deposited $5,000 in an account in the Sleepy Eye Savings and Loan Association standing in the name of "'Arry and Bing, as joint tenants." 'Arry retained the passbook for this account and did not tell Bing of the existence of the account.

[*266*]

(2) 'Arry placed another $5,000 in an envelope, sealed it and wrote with pen on the outside of the envelope, "This belongs to 'Arry and Bing, as joint tenants." 'Arry then placed this envelope in his safe deposit box. While at the bank, he mentioned to the teller that he had just made a gift to his son, so that his taxes would be reduced.

(3) 'Arry set up two more accounts in the Savings and Loan Association in the following names: "'Arry, in trust for Candy" and "'Arry, in trust for Ursula." He deposited $10,000 in each of these accounts, retained the passbooks and did not inform Candy or Ursula of his action.

(4) Shortly thereafter 'Arry executed a deed of 'Appy Acre, three acres of unimproved real estate he owned, to ". . . my brother, 'Enry, and my wife's daughter, Virna." After executing this deed, 'Arry recorded it with the Register of Deeds and then placed it in his safe deposit box. He wrote a letter to 'Enry and Virna, which provided in part: "This property, presently worth about $6,000, has great potential; and it is my intention to give this property to both of you in anticipation of your inheritance from me."

Virna was married, had one daughter, Julie, and, of course, did not reside with her mother. However, 'Arry desired to further demonstrate his affection for her, and some months after making the above transfers, 'Arry legally adopted Virna. Unfortunately, soon thereafter Virna was fatally injured in an auto accident. She left surviving her husband, Huck, and her daughter, Julie.

Some months later, while reading the advance sheets of the Supreme Court Reports, 'Arry suffered a massive heart attack and died. 'Arry left the following property:

(1) The residence of 'Arry and Ursula, Bedside Manor. This property was owned by 'Arry, Ursula and Bing, as tenants-in-common. It was situated on five acres of the choicest land in Sleepy Eye. It had an appraised value of $44,000, and was subject to a mortgage with a balance on the date of death of $20,000.

(2) The savings accounts 'Arry had created had increased in value as follows:

" 'Arry and Bing, as joint tenents"—$6,000 balance

" 'Arry, in trust for Candy"—$12,000 balance

" 'Arry, in trust for Ursula"—$12,000 balance

(3) The envelope in 'Arry's safe deposit box, marked "This belongs to 'Arry and Bing, as joint tenants," was found still containing $5,000.

(4) Other personal property (in excess of debts, taxes and expenses of administration) in the amount of $156,000.

Following receipt of 'Arry's letter regarding 'Appy Acre, 'Enry had erected a gasoline station on a corner of the property. This business was immediately successful, and at the date of 'Arry's death 'Appy Acre had a value of $60,000.

Shortly after 'Arry's death, the entire town of Sleepy Eye was shocked when Dastard arrived on the scene and claimed to be 'Arry's illegitimate son, entitled to a share of the estate. As proof of his claim, Dastard filed with the probate court a certified copy of a paternity decree entered by a court in another county declaring 'Arry Abinger of Sleepy Eye, Minnesota, to be the father of Dastard and providing for child support in the amount of $50 per month until Dastard reached the age of 18. The record of that proceeding indicates that 'Arry did not appear therein. Dastard is also able to prove, through old bank records, that 'Arry sent a check for $50 to Dastard's mother each month, beginning immediately after the entry of the paternity judgment and continuing until Dastard reached the age of 18.

You have been retained as attorney for Bing, who has been appointed administrator of his father's estate. Prepare for him a memorandum determining the proper distribution of all of 'Arry's property described above. Discuss the validity of all inter vivos transactions. Discuss the interest which any of the parties will take under the intestate succession laws. This memorandum should discuss all issues relevant to the determination of these shares. Specifically, what share of 'Arry's property are each of the following persons entitled to:

    (a) Ursula

    (b) Bing

    (c) Candy

    (d) Huck

    (e) Julie

    (f) 'Enry

    (g) Dastard

.   .   .   .   .   .

COMMENT: This real and personal property problem, rather than less-complex separate problems involving solely real or personal property law, is used here because it illustrates (1) how the law governing both types of property is usually involved in the estate-settlement situations so frequently handled by lawyers, and (2) the increasing use on law examinations of these more complex, issue-studded and multi-partied fact situations now frequently encountered in law practice. It is perhaps worth noting that, as here, examiners frequently select names for the parties in a problem with each name beginning with a different letter which can be conveniently substituted for the name without confusion when writing the answer, as in the following "A" answer.

ANSWERS TO PROPERTY (II)

GOOD "A" ANSWER

(1) The first transaction 'Arry (A) made was the joint savings account between himself and Bing (B). Gifts of joint accounts in banks have been held valid if the three requirements for gifts—donative intent, delivery, and acceptance by donee—are present. The delivery requirement here is taken care

of by the contract with the bank to deliver
the money to B on demand or at A's death.
This was an inter vivos gift as A was not
acting in contemplation of death. The acceptance by B is normally assumed and must
be almost expressly repudiated in order to
find "no acceptance". Thus, the main problem in this situation is A's donative intent.
This is somewhat of a gift of a future interest in that B gets the account when A dies.
A's keeping the passbook does not show no
donative intent because the nature of the
interest created by the gift allows both A
(and presumably B) to use the account while
they are alive. Thus, A's mere keeping of the
book is not necessarily inconsistent with the
requisite donative intent. These types of
gifts, then, are generally 'revocable' but are
still upheld, and treated as a gift to B of
what is left in the account when A dies.
So the retention of the passbook by A does
not wholly negate A's giving up of control
over the gift because of its nature. This
could be held a valid transfer.

(2) The second purported gift of $5000
cash to B but left in a sealed envelope in the
box is not as easy to establish. For in that
case, although acceptance would be assumed,
the delivery is difficult to find. Since A owns

the safe deposit box he has not really divested himself of control over this money—and
while A lives B cannot get at the money and
use it as he presumably could with the joint
account. Although delivery to a third person
(e. g. bank) for the donee can be a valid
delivery, as in the joint account case, this
putting money in the safe deposit box is not
really a delivery to the bank for B since A
still controls the box exclusively. The intention to give was present here, as it was
in the joint account gift, and is even clearer
because of A's declaration to the bank teller.
Perhaps this can also be treated as a gift of
a future interest to B. Perhaps if A's intent
to do this can be clearly shown the delivery
requirement can be lessened somewhat. The
main problem, though, is still that B can't get
at the money, as he could in the joint account
gift, and A has not given up any control.
But again, this may be seen as a present gift
of a future interest to B, giving him what is
left on the death of A. For this reason the
gift might perhaps be valid because of the
strong intent shown. This could not be held
an oral trust because there was no declaration of a trust—but perhaps it's valid anyway.

(3) The accounts set up in trust for Candy (C) and Ursula (U) are Totten Trusts. These have been held, in Minnesota, to be testamentary transfers and they are valid at A's death unless A has revoked them or done some other act of disaffirmance. Even though A did not tell C or U about the accounts they are still valid. It is not necessary to inform the donee in a Totten Trust. These have been recognized as valid for a long time because of the reliance placed on them by testators and others. Their effect on the intestate succession to A's property will be discussed later.

(4) The conveyance of 'Appy Acre to 'Enry (E) and Virna (V) probably could constitute an advancement as to V. Under Minnesota law, to have an advancement the testator must die wholly intestate (as A did) and the advancement must be set out in writing and expressed as an advancement. However, an advancement can only be made to a child or other lineal descendant. E, A's brother, is clearly not one of those, and at the time of the conveyance neither was V. The issue, then, is whether A's later adoption of V changes this and makes it an advancement as to her. When V was adopted she became, legally, the natural child of A in all

relevant aspects. The question is really whether to give a sort of "relation back" effect to the adoption and thus make the gift an advancement. (It clearly was a gift; there was acceptance, and also delivery even if the deed still was in A's control. The deed was recorded. Also, a strong intention to give was present because of A's letter to E and V. The fact that the recorded deed was not given to E and V should not invalidate it as a gift. Since the deed was recorded, that should amount to sufficient delivery. The reason for requiring delivery is to make it clear that the donor knew what he was doing. It is also evidentiary. The recording serves all of these purposes and makes it a valid delivery and gift.) The rationale behind advancements is to let an intestate give part of his property to his descendants early. Since that is what A was doing in regard to V, the fact that she only became his child by later adoption is of little importance. Thus, this should be an advancement to V, and since V died leaving her daughter, Julie (J), as issue, under Minn.Stat. § 525.53, the advancement is treated as going directly to J. E and V (J) would be deemed tenants-in-common—they are not joint tenants unless expressly stated as such—and the value of the advancement is the value expressed in the writing regardless of future developments, provided such value was a reasonable one at the time, and it is.

(5) In regard to the interests of these people after A's death and under intestate succession: How the residence of A and U passes depends upon its status as a homestead. In any event, B will keep his ⅓ as tenant-in-common and U will keep her ⅓. The problem is as to A's ⅓. Unless it comes within the first definition in Minn.Stat. § 510.02, which allows 80 acres as homestead in an unplatted municipality, it can't be wholly a homestead because it is larger than the ½ acre permitted for homesteads in platted municipalities. So, unless this is in an 80 acre area it passes as non-homestead real property. To the extent it is a homestead, U would get a life estate in A's ⅓ interest with remainder in fee to B, C and J.

The mortgage can't be exonerated out of estate assets because of Minn.Stat. § 525.442 —also the wife must sign a Security Mortgage. The Jones case said that a purchase-money mortgage can't be exonerated.

The Totten Trusts for C and U are included in valuing the estate to determine the wife's share but the wife takes her share out of estate assets first until she gets to the Totten Trust assets. Since one of the trusts is in her name, should this be included? It probably should be, for otherwise she would be overly benefitted. She would get her normal share and that is all she should get. A wanted to avoid taxes, not increase U's share of his estate.

Thus the shares taken by the parties are:

(a) U—gets furniture and household goods not exceeding $2000, and other personal property not exceeding $1000 under Minn. Stat. § 525.15(1), totalling $3000. Also, U gets ⅓ of the remaining assets ($156,000 plus Totten Trust assets of $24,000). Also, if Bedside Manor is a homestead, U gets a life estate in A's ⅓ interest. If not, she gets an outright ⅓ of A's ⅓ interest. U gets her Totten Trust, too.

(b) B—Bing gets the two gifts to him and ⅓ of the $96,000 remaining after U's share and the Totten Trusts are subtracted. Also, if Bedside Manor is a homestead B gets a ⅓ remainder in A's share after the life estate in U. If not, B gets ⅓ of A's share.

(c) C—Candy gets her Totten Trust plus ⅓ of the remaining $96,000 and the same interest in Bedside as B.

(d) H—Huck gets nothing since relatives by marriage get nothing.

(e) J—Julie, by representation, gets what her mother, Virna, would have had. Her advancement (½ of 'Appy Acre) is worth $3,000, since A declared in writing that the land was worth $6,000. As issue of Virna, A's adopted daughter, J gets ⅓ (less $3000) of the $96,000 ($30,000). Thus, B and C would actually get an extra $1,000 each. (C and B get $33,000 and J, $30,000)

(f) E—'Enry gets his ½ of 'Appy Acre, but nothing under intestate succession.

(g) D—Dastard gets nothing. By Minn. Stat. § 525.172 an illegitimate child can only inherit from a father who declares himself to be such. A paternity suit is not determinative. Even A's support of D and his mother is not enough to bring this case out of the statute, so D gets nothing.

.   .   .   .   .   .

MARGINAL ANSWER

(1) The joint savings account in the names of 'Arry and Bing would not be a valid and completed inter vivos gift. For such a gift to be valid, there must be donative intent, delivery, and acceptance. Here, there was no

delivery so there could be no acceptance. Further, the lack of delivery raises doubts as to whether there was a donative intent.

For delivery, there need not be an actual transfer of the property, but there must at least be some kind of symbolic delivery, i. e. the key to a safe deposit box, or a passbook for a bank account. There must be some act by which the donor divests himself of control over the gift. Here there was no such delivery, actual or constructive. 'Arry did not divest himself of any control over the account. He did not give the book to Bing, or to a third person to hold for Bing (which would also be a valid delivery), nor did he even inform anyone of the gift. Not only then, was there lack of delivery but we cannot know his actual intent. Had he even told someone of his action we would at least have some manifestation of his intention, even though this alone would hardly be conclusive. Further, because he retained control over this property, he could revoke the gift at any time, and this also is inconsistent with the concept of a valid inter vivos gift, which is irrevocable.

Normally, a joint bank account is a proper inter vivos gift, but absent the clear expression of intent, and absent either an actual or a constructive delivery, this gift could not be held valid.

(2) The second gift, in the envelope, would, I think, be sufficiently definite to constitute a valid inter vivos gift. Here, by sealing the money in the envelope, he did manifest an intention to give up possession of it. His comment to the bank teller would be further evidence to prove that there was donative intent. Although he did not deliver the key to his son, I believe that the sealing of the envelope was sufficient evidence that he did give up control of the money. Telling a third person of a gift is good enough as an expression of intent, although in this case it was not as reliable as telling his attorney, for instance. Again, a joint tenancy is a proper subject of a gift.

(3) These trusts are valid gifts also, in the form of Totten Trusts. True, 'Arry still retains control over them as Trustee, and has complete authority to add to or deplete them as he wishes, but when he dies, whatever is left in them will go to the beneficiaries of the Trusts. Here again, there is a problem with delivery, but by putting the money in a trust fund, he no longer has ownership

of the property, although he does have possession and control. Putting it in Trust could be considered an objective manifestation of his intention to give up the possession of the money. As always, when he himself (the donor) is the Trustee, there is a problem with intent, especially when he did not inform the beneficiaries of his action. It is one of the borderline cases. But, to benefit those for whom the Trust appears to have been intended, I could hold that this is a valid inter vivos gift.

(4) The deed to 'Appy Acre would also be considered a valid transaction as to Virna but not as to 'Enry because an advancement can only go to lineal descendants, and not to a brother. Again, 'Arry did not deliver the actual deed to 'Enry and Virna, but kept it within his control in his safety box. He did have the deed executed and recorded, and in fact even wrote to the beneficiaries explaining his actions. Thus, his donative intent was apparent, and it would seem that by recording the deed, the delivery was sufficient also. This method of delivery should be every bit as sufficient as that in the *Mills* case. There would be a presumption here that because the land was given to them together, they would be tenants-in-common.

This, however, appears different from the other gift, because by his language, in the latter, it is an advancement. Thus, they will have to account for it if they want to collect under a will or a statutory share when he dies, whereas the other donees do not have to account for their gifts. When the time comes for them to "bring it into hotchpot" the value of the land will be that at the time the gift was made, and not the value when 'Arry dies. Thus, if the land increases in value, it will be to the benefit of Virna and 'Enry. Since Virna predeceased 'Arry, her heirs will have to bring the gift "into hotchpot", if they want to receive her share of 'Arry's estate, which they will do even if she was an adopted child. An adopted child will take a share in an estate as though she were a legitimate child. Thus, her heirs could take by representation.

Now, as to the shares that each person could get: At Common Law, Ursula, his wife, would get her ⅓ dower interest of all lands of which he was seized at any time during the marriage, provided such lands would be inheritable by issue of that marriage. She would get this as a life estate. Then, unless she had consented to the signing of the deed to 'Enry and Virna, she would get a ⅓ life estate in 'Appy Acre. Also, she would get a ⅓ life estate in 'Arry's ⅓ of Bedside Manor, and would then still have her own share of Bedside Manor. Then, except for the other gifts which were discussed as being valid, the whole rest of the estate would go to the eldest son; being Bing.

Under Minnesota Intestate Succession Laws:

(a) Ursula—takes a life estate in the homestead, with remainder to children or issue in equal shares.

—his wearing apparel; $2000 of household goods and $1000 of other personal property.

—⅓ of rest of the personal property, or $52,000.

—⅓ of all real property of which he was seized during marriage unless she consented to the sale of it, i. e. 'Appy Acre.

(b) Bing—remainder in homestead

—⅓ of remaining ⅔, or ⅔ of remaining personal property.

(c) Candy—dead, but her share goes to Julie—Minn.Stat. § 259.29.

(d) Huck—O

(e) Julie—takes her mother's share by representation, so will get ⅜ of the personal property.

(f) 'Enry—O

(g) Dastard—will inherit his share, ⅜, according to Minn.Stat. § 525.172.

.   .   .   .   .   .

COMMENT: This answer, in its discussion of the four inter vivos gifts, is well-written and fairly well reasoned, although not nearly as accurate or complete in its analysis and understanding of the law as the "A" answer. The mere fact that this answer reaches different conclusions as to the validity of some of the gifts would make no difference in the grading if the understanding of applicable law had been accurate and the reasoning and application to the facts sound, since validity of the transfers is questionable and properly arguable either way. The answer deteriorates badly, however, when it comes to the question of the intestate distribution of the estate; what each party would be entitled to receive, and why. This part is largely some hasty, and in some respects inaccurate conclusions with little analysis or careful reasoning. In many places it merely summarizes the provisions of the statutes (which the writer had before him) without careful application to each party or the specific conclusions requested in the problem. As a result it would receive a minimum "C" grade at best.

PROPERTY (III)

(1 hour)

You arrive at your law office one cool June morning and discover in your mail the following letter from your client, Senator Nelson Stonedfellow, who is a highly regarded young member of the Minnesota legislature:

Dear Counsellor:

This session I am chairman of an interim subcommittee established to consider and recommend reforms in the landlord and tenant law of this State. The following five bills have been referred to our subcommittee. Would you prepare for me a memorandum analyzing and evaluating this proposed legislation. Specifically, would you discuss (a) the changes, if any, these bills would make in present Minnesota law or the common law; and (b) whether or not such changes, if any, are desirable.

I. A BILL FOR AN ACT

Subd. 1: In every lease or license of residential premises, the lessor or licensor covenants:

(a) That the premises and all common areas are fit for the use intended by the parties.

(b) To keep the premises in reasonable repair during the term of the lease or license, and to comply with the applicable health and safety laws of the state and of the local unit of government where the premises are located, except when the disrepair or violation of the applicable health or safety laws has been caused by the tenant's willful or irresponsible conduct.

Subd. 2: The parties to the lease or license may modify the obligations imposed by Subd. 1(b) where the lease or license has a current term of at least one year, but may not modify the obligations of Subd. 1(a).

Subd. 3: The provisions of this section shall be liberally construed, and the privilege of a prospective lessee or licensee to inspect the premises before concluding a lease or license shall not defeat his right to have the benefit of the covenants established herein.

II.   A BILL FOR AN ACT

Subd. 1: The lessee or occupant of any building or part thereof which, without fault or neglect on his part, shall become untenantable or unfit for occupancy is not liable thereafter to pay rent to the lessor or owner thereof. The lessee shall not be required, as a condition of asserting the benefits of this section, to abandon possession of the premises within a reasonable time after the said premises are alleged to have become untenantable or unfit for occupancy; but the lessee may, if he so desires, remain in possession of the said premises until such time as it shall be finally determined by the proper court or agreed to by the lessor that the premises are untenantable or unfit for occupancy, provided that the lessee shall abandon possession of the premises within a reasonable time after such determination or agreement. The lessee shall remain liable for the rent until such time as he shall abandon possession of the premises.

Subd. 2: Where only a portion of the leased premises shall become untenantable or unfit for occupancy within the provisions of subd. 1, or where the leased premises shall become untenantable or unfit for occupancy within the meaning of subd. 1 for only certain limited but recurring periods of time, the lessee may, upon application to the proper court, receive an abatement of the rent due for the leased premises. Nothing contained in subd. 2 of this section shall preclude a lessee from abandoning possession of the premises and being excused from further payment of rent as provided in subd. 1 hereof.

Subd. 3: A building or part thereof shall be deemed to be untenantable or unfit for occupancy within the provisions of subd. 1, where such building or part thereof is in violation of any health, safety, housing or building code or ordinance.

III. A BILL FOR AN ACT

When any lessee of real estate holds over and retains possession thereof after expiration of the term of the lease without express contract with the owner, no tenancy for any other period than the shortest interval between the times of payment of rent under the terms of the expired lease shall be implied.

IV. A BILL FOR AN ACT

A lessor's duty to maintain in reasonable repair the areas used in common by the lessees of a multiple dwelling shall include the duty to provide adequate lighting.

V. A BILL FOR AN ACT

Subd. 1: It shall be a defense to an action for restitution of the premises following the alleged termination of a tenancy by notice to quit for the lessee to prove by a fair preponderance of the evidence that:

(a) The alleged termination was intended as a penalty for the lessee's attempt to secure or enforce rights under a lease or contract, oral or written, or under the laws of the state, any of its governmental subdivisions, or of the United States.

(b) The alleged termination was intended as a penalty for the lessee's report to a governmental authority of the lessor's violation of any health, safety, housing or building codes or ordinances.

(c) The alleged termination was intended as retaliation for any lawful act arising out of the tenancy.

If the notice to quit was served within ninety days of the date of any act of the tenant coming within the terms of paragraphs (a), (b) or (c) of this Subsection, the burden of proving that the notice to quit was not served for a retaliatory purpose shall rest with the lessor.

Subd. 2: In any proceeding for the restitution of premises upon the ground of non-payment of rent, it shall be a defense thereto if the lessee establishes by a preponderance of the evidence that the lessor increased the lessee's rent as a penalty for any lawful act of the lessee as described in Subd. 1 of this section, providing that the lessee tender to the Court the amount of rent due under his original obligation.

Best wishes for a happy summer.

Sincerely,
Senator Nelson Stonedfellow

Write a reply to your client.

. . . . . .

COMMENT: Lawyers frequently are employed (or volunteer) to draft proposed legislation to alter or improve existing law. The time pressures and requirements of an ordinary law exam preclude effective testing of students' ability and skill in the use of language in the careful and exacting task of drafting a suitable statute. This must be tested by other methods. However, lawyers are sometimes asked, as in the foregoing problem, to analyze proposed drafts of bills and submit memoranda outlining the effects, advantages and shortcomings of the proposals. This type of problem is suitable for the ordinary law exam. It involves the same kinds of legal knowledge, understanding, analysis, issue-recognition and reasoning as are necessary in answering problems involving the determination of rights or liabilities under existing law, but requires a different application through evaluating the proposed changes in the law. This type of problem also tests a student's ability to read statutory language with the extreme care, accuracy and thoroughness that are necessary for its analysis and application.

.   .   .   .   .   .

ANSWERS TO PROPERTY (III)

GOOD "A" ANSWER

I.   The first bill imposes on lessors (L) implied warranties as to the condition and repair of leased premises more extensive than those under common law or present Minnesota law. At common law L's duty extended only to latent defects known to him at the time of the lease and not likely to come to tenant's (T's) attention. In such cases L is liable in damages to T if the failure to tell T results in injury from the defect. There is also a warranty, in a lease of a furnished place for immediate occupancy and for a short term, that the premises are safe for the intended use. Also, L has a duty to T to inspect and use reasonable care with respect to the safety of common areas of use. Except for these, the rule is generally *caveat emptor*. Also, unless L covenants to repair, the duty of repair falls upon T. T is not a guarantor of the condition of the premises but he is liable for waste. L is presently required to comply with applicable health and safety laws but is usually able to get around them. This is the basic common law.

The proposed Bill I changes these rules with respect to residential property only. Commercial property would still be governed wholly by common law. The implied warranty imposed in Subd. 1(a) is probably desirable. In modern context L knows much more than T does about the condition of the leased premises. It is a reasonable assumption that T is relying on L to have the premises in a safe and suitable condition for their intended use. Thus the imposition of an implied warranty of their fitness would seem to be a desirable change in the law.

L's duty to repair under Subd. 1(b) is a definite change from common law under which L has such duty only when he covenants to repair. This proposed duty may be desirable economically because L could probably do all repairs a little cheaper than T could. But in some areas Ls are poor and might not be able to afford this repair burden. Thus, this burden, with that in Subd. 1(a) would probably result in general rent increases. This burden might also interfere with T's privacy because L would have to be allowed to enter frequently for inspection and repairs. But if the purpose of Bill I is to bring about better housing conditions, putting the repair burden on L would probably be more conducive to this. Subd. 1(b) relieves L from this repair duty if T causes the disrepair wilfully or irresponsibly, and the Bill should probably state that T is responsible, or at least liable to L, for such disrepair. It is also doubtful whether the Bill should relieve L from obligation to fix code violations even where caused by T's willful conduct. This defeats the purpose of the code in maintaining minimum standards. Imposing a fine on T but requiring L to remedy code violations might be appropriate when caused by T.

Subd. 2 is desirable in preventing modification of the warranty in Subd. 1(a) since Ts would have no bargaining power. Permitting modification of the repair obligation under Subd. 1(b) only in leases for a year or more also seems desirable for the same reason. Ts leasing for a year or more presumably are in a position to bargain with respect to repairs, so this option should be permitted.

Subd. 3 precluding waiver by tenant's inspection seems necessary to effectuate the purposes of Subd. 1.

It is proper to exclude commercial property because commercial tenants are generally able to protect themselves in lease bargaining.

Perhaps there should be a clause making L liable for tort damages caused by his breach of the obligations in Subd. 1.

II. Proposed Bill II is similar to present Minn.Stat. § 504.05 but, unlike that section, does not permit a contrary provision in the lease. Under § 504.05, T now has to abandon promptly in order to use the statutory defense of constructive eviction, except, possibly, if T sues L in equity. This proposed Bill II may be a bit overbroad. It may be allowing T to abandon for any condition if it's bad enough, and would change the common law requirement that the untenantable condition be caused by L's affirmative act and that the premises must be promptly abandoned by T. Under Bill II T can remain in possession until legal determination of untenantability. This is good because present law leaves T in a dilemma as to what to do if there is doubt on this. If T abandons possession he may be in default if the condition is found not to make the premises untenantable. If he remains in possession he may lose his right to abandon. Subd. 1 of Bill II seems desirable.

Subd. 2 provides a new remedy since there is no present doctrine of partial constructive eviction and it has been little used and little recognized. Perhaps this proposal is sound because it lets T stay in possession (if he wants to) and still get a rent reduction because of the problem. This gives T a remedy where before he had none and could only vacate and incur the risk of being in default. A partial constructive eviction can be just as devastating to T as a whole one and T should have a remedy for this.

In subd. 3, the definition of untenantable should not be limited to code violations. The definition should cover any condition that makes the premises in fact untenantable with code violations constituting untenantability per se.

Bill II substantially expands Minn.Stat. § 504.05 and provides T with an affirmative remedy for constructive eviction which now is primarily a defense to L's suit for rent. This Bill probably does away with the requirement of an affirmative act by L causing untenantability and also eliminates the requirement of prompt abandonment by T which is a good idea. Perhaps the Bill should permit T to get damages for moving expense and higher rent elsewhere if L caused the abandonment affirmatively.

III. Bill III would amend and broaden Minn.Stat. § 504.07, which applies only to "urban real estate", by making it applicable to any real estate, urban or rural. Presently, a tenant of rural real estate who holds over is subject to the common law rule which permits L to treat the hold-over as creating a tenancy for a whole year (under a year-to-year lease) rather than for the shortest interval between rent payments. The common law rule imposes a penalty and should be changed since it may not help either L or T. Bill III also gets rid of the problem of deciding what is rural and what is urban real estate.

IV. Bill IV merely adds to L's duties a specific duty to provide adequate lighting in common areas. This has not been required under present Minnesota statutes or common law. It seems clear that if L's common law duty is to take reasonable measures to keep common areas safe, a duty of adequate lighting should be included. This Bill will add it and this seems desirable. It is reasonable since L is in control of common areas.

V.   Bill V provides T with a defense in restitution actions that does not exist under
Minnesota law.   Something like this has
been adopted in the District of Columbia but
not in Minnesota.   It is desirable to the extent that it gives T a defense where L's eviction is only because of T's attempt to enforce
the rights specified in subd. 1(a) or (b).
These are rights of T which should be upheld
and T should be given remedies to help him.
At present, a T's major protection is in the
housing codes, etc., and if he can be evicted
every time he mentions them or reports
them the codes will become useless and the
protection will be gone.   Thus, in order to
help Ts and to fulfill the policy underlying
the adoption of the codes (a) and (b) are
good.

However, paragraph (c) sweeps a little
too broadly.   This means that if notice to
quit is given within 90 days of any lawful
act by T the burden is on L to show that
eviction is non-retaliatory.   This is a bit
severe.   Perhaps it should be restricted to
evictions within 90 days of an exercise by
T of the rights enumerated in (a) or (b)
with the burden on T to prove retaliation in
evictions within 90 days from any other act

on T's part. The same idea could be incorporated in subd. 2 with the burden on L to prove non-retaliation if the rent raise occurred within 90 days after T exercised a right enumerated in subd. 1(a) or (b).

The problem is that subd. 1(c) is so broad that L might never be able to get T out, or raise his rent, if he could not meet the burden of proof.

The idea of helping T in some way in this area covered by Bill V is a good one and the provisions in subd. 1(a) and (b) are useful for this purpose. Putting the burden of proof on L here is also useful—it makes him think twice—but (c) goes too far.

.   .   .   .   .   .

MARGINAL ANSWER

Ostensibly Bill I, subd. 1, would make Landlord liable for common areas and reasonable repair of buildings, complying with applicable health laws (except for wilfull misconduct by tenant). This does absolutely nothing new in the law except to place the force of statutory law behind prior case law decisions. Tied in with Subd. 2 the situation remains the same. By letting the Landlord put in exculpatory clauses removing him from liability you are doing nothing. Subd. 1 is a common law requirement establishing for common stairways a duty to repair. The avoidable consequences doctrine probably could no longer be used but this was not very useful anyway. The bargaining power of the Landlord is so great that to allow exculpatory clauses in the lease defeats the supposed purpose of the rule requiring an obligation to keep in repair. Inspection is part of the current law, and even if exculpatory clauses were not used and landlords had to repair, they would raise the rents of the people who can't afford better housing, and move them out. This certainly would not be a solution to the poor, impoverished tenant's problems.

Another problem here is who determines what a tenant's "wilful or irresponsible conduct" is. If this is interpreted to mean simply non-feasance then no change by the bill will have occurred. Is misfeasance of the landlord the criteria used to determine his duty of reasonable repair? Does he have to make some affirmative act? If he does there's no change in the law.

Bill II, subd. 1 would change Minn.Stat. § 504.05 and allow T to remain on the premises and continue paying rent until a court can decide whether the premises are untenantable. This would be a major step forward in attempting to work out problems between T and L. It takes the guesswork out of whether T should move or not, using the court as a declaratory forum in deciding the outcome of the situation. This brings in the theory of *interdependence* which is so lacking in the property law and uses more of a contract theory of *interdependence*. T and L are bound together. If T stays he pays rent and if the property is found to be untenantable the court can determine the result.

Subd. 2 allows, statutorily, for partial constructive evictions, following a very few cases on the subject. It allows for abatement so that the all-or-nothing risk of leaving premises is not needed. It retains the right to abandon, giving the lessee a better choice of alternatives than before (i. e. no choice).

Bill III is the same as Minn.Stat. § 504.07. This discriminates between people paying at large intervals of time and is arbitrary.

Bill IV. This is good because the common law did not demand that the landlord keep common areas well lighted (no light at all required). This is a simple solution to a long and unnecessary risk under common law.

Bill V. This section has been partly adopted in Minneapolis. The penalty clause is an effective weapon against any complaint but it may in the long run place an undue burden on the Landlord. The Bill implies that *anytime* within 90 days of any act of tenants coming forward the Landlord would be denied the right to raise rent or give notice to quit. This might put a burden on Landlord because if Landlord gave notice or raised rent, tenant could place a report and place the burden on Landlord to prove that it was not a penalty. This is too harsh.

As Benjamin Cardozo said, (which is very applicable to Landlord laws) "We do not pick our rules of law full blossomed from the trees".

We must slowly work for a more equitable arrangement in Landlord-Tenant Property Law.

.   .   .   .

COMMENT: This answer obviously discloses the writer's failure in several respects to read carefully the language of the various Bills

and note changes made by them in existing law. Also, of course, it fails to discuss a number of the questions and policies involved in the proposed legislation which the "A" answer brings out. It is thus superficial and in some respects erroneous as to existing law, and at best only a marginally adequate answer.

PROCEDURE (I)

(30 minutes)

A state statute of limitations for torts is two years; for contracts, three years. It provides also that when a complaint is dismissed voluntarily or by order of a court, a new complaint based on the same occurrence can be brought within six months. But it also provides that amendments to complaints do not relate back (as under the Federal Rules).

On May 1, 1969, Adams brought suit against Baker Co., a manufacturer of furniture, alleging that he had bought a chair made by Baker Co. on May 1, 1967, and that it had broken under him the same day, seriously injuring him, and charging that the chair had been negligently made. The suit was brought in the United States District Court for the District in the above-mentioned state on grounds of diversity of citizenship. (You may assume jurisdiction was proper). Baker Co. moved to dismiss on the grounds that no action of negligence could be brought because it was not in privity with Adams. Adams thereupon dismissed the action on May 15, 1969.

Adams brought another suit against Baker Co. in the same court on November 1, 1969, alleging breach of warranty in connection with the same accident. On May 20, 1970, Adams moved to amend his complaint to add a count based on negligence.

Baker Co. objected to the motion to amend on two grounds: First, that the negligence count was barred by the dismissal of the first complaint. Second, that the negligence count was barred by the statute of limitations.

How should the court rule?

.   .   .   .   .   .

ANSWERS TO PROCEDURE (1)

GOOD "A" ANSWER

The defendant pleaded affirmatively that no action of negligence could be brought for lack of privity and Adams dismissed. Presumably the dismissal was voluntary and in compliance with the terms of Rule 41(a) and, if so, would be without prejudice to his claim. If he had not dismissed and the court had ordered involuntary dismissal, the dismissal would be prejudicial. Thus the objection by Baker to the subsequent motion to amend the complaint to include negligence would be without grounds on contention number one. (There was no prejudice under the Federal Rules.) Nor is there any reason to believe there would be prejudice to plaintiff's claim in the dismissal because of the state statute which allows a subsequent complaint.

What the court ought to do about the running of the statute of limitations is to hold that the defendant is not allowed to amend because justice does not so require under rule 15(a). The state statute of limitations was designed to protect defendant against stale claims and specifically provides only a six month extension of time to renew the original suit with an amended complaint. Here the extension is coupled with the provision that amendments do not relate back as they do under the Federal Rules. The state has a substantial interest in barring stale claims. Defendant is attempting to assert a negligence claim 18 months after the running of the original statute of limitations on it by a mixture of Federal rules and state law thus thwarting the intent and purpose of the state statute of limitations. While defendant did have notice of the possibility of a negligence claim, plaintiff ought not now be allowed to manipulate the rules to the extent of thwarting the state's interest in preventing stale claims. The court ought to deny the motion to amend on the running of the statute of limitations in the negligence claim.

.   .   .   .   .   .

MARGINAL ANSWER

Rule 41(a) provides that a voluntary dismissal by a plaintiff does not act as an adjudication on the merits and the Federal Courts have allowed a leave to amend. This is similar to the state rule and there is little conflict between the two rules. A voluntary dismissal thus does not act as res judicata to another action. However, if a plaintiff does not amend within the time allowed by the court the motion does act as res judicata. Since plaintiff had not submitted the amendment within the proper time it would be barred from admission.

A conflict arises between Federal and state law as to whether the amendment could relate back. The cases dealing with state law in federal courts would probably say that federal rule 15(c) was applicable and the amendment did relate back. However, a standard of reasonableness in making amendments would be applied. If the court wouldn't accept the state six months amendment period, it would appear that an amendment submitted over a year later, if allowed, would defeat the purpose of the statute of limitations and thus would not be allowed to relate back.

.   .   .   .   .   .

COMMENT: The question is a simple one, and does not call for an extensive answer. The good "A" answer clearly separates the two issues, and answers each succinctly. In the second and more controversial issue, the anomaly of mixing federal and state law is clearly pointed out.

The marginal answer seems to confuse the two issues. It's discussion of the first issue appears to mix Rule 41, the amendment problem of the second issue, and the doctrine (not applicable in federal courts) that a dismissal with leave to amend requires amendment. In its discussion of the second issue, the conclusion is very ambiguous. Note that the sentence "However, a standard of reasonableness in making amendments would be applied," does not indicate which result the application of such a standard would point to.

PROCEDURE (II)

(45 minutes)

Fox brought suit against Gander in a Federal District Court alleging that Gander and Hare had entered a contract under which Hare paid Gander $1,000 in return for Gander's promise to pay Fox for any damage suffered by Fox in the course of certain blasting operations which Hare was conducting on land adjoining Fox's whether Hare was legally liable or not, and further alleging that Hare's blasting had wrecked Fox's house, damaging him in the amount of $12,000, which sum Fox had demanded from Gander and had been refused.

Gander's attorneys jumped quickly into action, and took statements from Hare, as well as from Kanga and Lynx who had been present when the contract was made; Hare died before his statement could be reduced to an affidavit, but Lynx made an affidavit that it had been expressly agreed between Gander and Hare that the contract was intended to create a right only in Hare and that no enforceable right in Fox was intended or created. Accompanying Lynx's affidavit with his own to the same effect, Gander moved for summary judgment.

Fox has served written interrogatories upon Gander demanding the statements obtained from Hare, Kanga, and Lynx, but Gander has refused to comply. Fox has not taken Gander's deposition, because he assumes it would be substantially in accord with Gander's affidavit. Fox is prepared to make an affidavit that Hare told him that he was protected by the contract. Fox believes he could shake Lynx's story, but Lynx is in another state several hundred miles away; while Kanga has privately told Fox that Gander's story of the contract is incorrect, he refuses to sign an affidavit.

What problems is Fox faced with, and what should he do?

.   .   .   .   .   .

ANSWERS TO PROCEDURE (II)

GOOD "A" ANSWER

Fox's immediate problem is to survive Gander's motion for summary judgment. Affidavits under Rule 56 have to be made on personal knowledge and must set forth such facts as would be admissible in evidence. The affidavit Fox says he is prepared to make does not fit these criteria, for, since Hare is dead and never was a party to the action, statements by Fox of what Hare said should be considered hearsay. Therefore Fox's affidavit alone would not be enough to create a genuine issue as to a material fact.

Under 56 (c) Fox has to come up with some evidence, affidavits, etc., to show there is a genuine issue as to material facts. He can't just rest on his pleadings.

Fox should try to get Hare's statement, for one thing, from Gander, since Hare is now dead. Gander will counter that this is his work product and not discoverable. A problem arises in that Hare died before he had a chance to reduce it to an affidavit. If this will force Gander's attorney to act as a witness, then this statement is absolutely privileged, and Fox won't be able to get this statement. But query whether this is true. It appears that Gander's attorneys were taking it in the form of an affidavit. Was everything done except the signing? It appears that this is a major problem. If Hare *had* in fact signed it, it would be discoverable due to "super" good cause that is here. Hare's statement will not stop the summary judgment, but may lead to further evidence.

Concerning Kanga's affidavit, Fox won't be able to get that from Gander's attorneys because Kanga is available and "super" good cause isn't met as required in the new Rule 26(b)3. The same is probably true of Lynx's affidavit too, even though he is several hundred miles away. It is still possible for Fox to get their story himself. First he should use Rule 34 and if Gander still refuses, Fox should seek a court order to compel Gander's attorney to hand over a copy of Hare's statement. He might get it.

Fox should try and get a favorable deposition from Lynx. A deposition will be the only way he can really dig into Lynx's story and cross-examine him in a sense. The problem here is, Lynx is several hundred miles away. Nonetheless, Fox should go to the expense and get Lynx's deposition. For this, he should serve notice on Lynx and Gander now.

Kanga refuses to sign an affidavit, even though his testimony will apparently be very valuable to Fox. Fox should depose him, again serving proper notice on Kanga's and Gander's attorneys. It seems that Kanga *may* refuse to say anything or even show up. Therefore Fox should, after giving notice, get a subpoena to require him to attend. If he refuses to answer any or all of the questions given in the deposition, Fox should apply for an order compelling discovery. The court will probably grant it here. This will probably be sufficient to get out of him the necessary and favorable information which he has, for he is faced with a possible contempt citation if he still refuses.

Kanga's deposition here alone would almost assuredly be sufficient for Fox to successfully defend against Gander's motion for summary judgment. Also added to this is the possibly favorable deposition of Lynx, and the slim, though real possibility of obtaining from Gander's attorneys Hare's statement. This, it may turn out, won't be really helpful but there certainly is the possibility.

Fox immediately should request a continuance on the motion for summary judgment, to permit him to get these depositions and helpful evidence.

Fox may also try to defeat the motion by showing that evidence exists that he would have at trial, but can't yet get, as per Rule 56 (f). Probably the request for a continuance is the better alternative though.

.   .   .   .   .   .

MARGINAL ANSWER

I. Fox is faced with the problem of how to obtain Hare's deposition.

II. Also the problem of how to get Lynx's deposition while he is out of the jurisdiction.

III. As to the "work product" of the lawyer for Gander:

Whether or not Fox can obtain the deposition of Hare, before his death, from Gander's attorney. Under rule 26 one can obtain work product of another lawyer if he is unable to get the information himself. The *Hickman* "good cause" requirement would be met under these circumstances since Hare is dead. As to the refusal of Gander to turn over the depositions of Kanga and Lynx, Fox will be unable to obtain them from Gander. In regard to Kanga's refusal, Fox can move for a court order under rule 37(a) (4).

In order for Fox to obtain the deposition of Lynx, he will have to use rule 49d(1) (2) but it has to be within 40 miles of the court issuing the subpoena.

.   .   .   .   .   .

COMMENT: Contrast the first sentence of the "A" answer with the entire marginal answer, which ignores the summary judgment problem. The problem obviously involves numerous discovery issues, but they are clearly centered on the specific problem of "How to meet the summary judgment motion?"

In the marginal answer, note also that the writer has attempted a sketchy outline of the issues, but has clearly not thought them out, since issues I and III are essentially the same. In his last paragraph, when possibly pressed for time, he has focussed on a very minor requirement (and has misstated it!).

CONSTITUTIONAL LAW (I)

(Open book exam—One hour)

In the State of Gopher the State Board of Education has in recent years increased the requirements in secondary education, including expansion of the science and language offerings and in library holdings and science laboratories. This has placed severe financial strains on non-public high schools which must meet these requirements in order to remain accredited and hence eligible to satisfy the state compulsory school attendance laws. As a result of the increased costs a few parochial high schools terminated their operations; when it seemed that more might do so the state legislature enacted a law authorizing local school boards to reimburse parents up to 50% of the tuition costs paid for sending their children to private accredited high schools within the state, including church-connected schools.

In Virginia, Gopher, the high school operated by the Roman Catholic Church educates 40% of the high school children. On May 1, 1970, the Church decided to terminate its high school effective September 1, 1971, in order to have adequate funds to maintain high quality education in the parochial grade school. The Virginia School Board ascertained (1) that parents were then paying $300 per year tuition for each child in the Church high school, and (2) that the Church would continue its high school if it could double the tuition to $600 but concluded that it could not increase the tuition parents must pay without loss of revenue due to withdrawal of children. The School Board then authorized the School District to reimburse parents up to 50% of the tuition fees paid for sending their children to an accredited private high school in the state, including church connected schools, but not to exceed 50% of the tuition or $300 per child, whichever was lower. The reimbursement was to be paid to the parent upon presenting to the School District a receipt for the tuition.

A taxpayer asks your senior partner to challenge the validity of the School Board action as applied to reimbursement of tuition paid to Catholic Church schools. Your partner asks you for a memorandum thoroughly analyzing the problem and giving your opinion as to the probable ruling in the U. S. Supreme Court if the proposed case reaches that Court. If any factual investigation is needed, advise your partner what facts you

need to investigate and what their relevance
may be in resolving the issue.

    .   .   .   .   .   .

**COMMENT: This type of problem does not
involve the recognition and resolution of numerous issues and sub-issues. It involves
only two or three basic constitutional issues
but requires in-depth analysis both of the applicable constitutional policies developed in
the cases dealing with those issues and the
real purposes and effects of the School Board
action, plus careful, plausible reasoning in
applying the policies in light of those purposes and effects. A mere "issue-spotting"
answer with cursory analysis is not appropriate here. Students must recognize that different types of problems require different
emphasis in the answers.**

    .   .   .   .   .   .

ANSWERS TO CONSTITUTIONAL LAW (I)

GOOD "A" ANSWER

The general test of constitutionality in the
area of financial aid to parochial schools was
outlined in Board of Education v. Allen

(1968): If either the purpose or primary effect of the enactment is the advancement or inhibition of religion, then the enactment exceeds the scope of legislative power as circumscribed by the Constitution; to withstand the Establishment Clause (1st Amendment) there must be a secular purpose and primary effect that neither advances nor inhibits religion. On this test the Court upheld the payment of public funds to buy textbooks for parochial schools.

A state has broad power to legislate for the public welfare, subject only to the strictures that the expenditure must be for a public purpose and that it must meet the 14th Amendment due process grounds of reasonableness. Only rarely has the Court struck down state expenditure statutes because they were not for a public purpose. On due process grounds the Court has consistently ruled that the state statute needs only a rational basis, and that when the state legislature has had rational grounds for an expenditure in the public interest, the Court will not second-guess the legislature on public interest, wisdom, or need.

Hence, on due process grounds the Court would most likely uphold the state action here, and with good reason. For a long time the Court engaged in second-guessing the states and the federal government on economic legislation. Public interest determination is much more a legislative fact question than a judicial fact. Legislatures are made to engage in policy issues and have greater access to information than do courts.

Besides due process, the 1st Amendment Establishment Clause and Free Exercise Clause, applicable to the states through the 14th Amendment, have a bearing on the parochial aid problem here.

First, as to the statute increasing educational requirements, which resulted in financial strain on private high schools, the argument may be made that this statute deprived Catholics of the right to free exercise of their religion, since the state now made it too expensive for them to go to church schools. This argument has no merit because (1) the requirements applied to all schools, the majority of which were likely public, so it was non-discriminatory; (2) the secular purpose and primary effect are obvious—to increase the quality of education of all youth.

Before dealing with the second aspect of the problem—the financial tuition aid to pa-

rochial schools—some facts should be known.
First, the proportion of parochial schools to
other private schools is important, for if there
are *no* other private schools, then a strong
argument is available that substance rules
over form, and that despite the form of granting aid to *all* private schools, the substance
is aid only to parochial schools; and that the
real purpose was therefore to aid the church.
Second, the proportion of tuition in church
schools that is used primarily for "secular"
education and the proportion used for what
may properly be called religious education, if
these are separable, is important. If over
half the tuition is for religious education,
then it might be argued that the state aid
is directly advancing religion.

It is clear that a state has a great interest
in education. To this end the state made education compulsory and made public education
available. Presumably, the state could have
as easily merely given financial aid to persons to seek a private education, but chose
not to do so.

Here the state has determined that financial aid to parents to reimburse them for 50%
of the tuition costs in private schools is in
the public interest. The aid is to go to all

parents who send their children to private schools. The state has not singled out church schools for support except in-so-far as they constitute private schools. Absent other facts the purpose appears to be purely secular—to make available better education to all children, irrespective of religion.

Arguably the statute is aiding religion. It is contributing to the support of religion because funds formally granted for educational purposes enable parochial schools to remain open for religious purposes. But I think that the Court would consider this aid to religion to be only incidental, provided the 50% of tuition did not amount to more than the fair cost of the secular educational benefits the children received. I believe the primary effect is secular.

Because a church has gratuitously undertaken the general education of a portion of the public does not mean that when the state undertakes this burden, the state is aiding religion. It is more like the church continuing to aid the state.

In providing this aid the state is not setting up a church, is not coercing the public to go to church, is not preferring any religion or non-religion and no religious activity is being supported. The law is merely extending an approved educational benefit to all regardless of religious belief. I believe the Court would uphold the aid program.

.   .   .   .   .   .

COMMENT: This is a well-organized, excellently written answer. It deals with the relevant constitutional law issues involved, explains the applicable case-law and policies involved, analyzes in some depth the purpose and effect of the challenged action taken by the Board of Education, presents good arguments and reasoning applying the legal requirements and reaches very plausible conclusions.

.   .   .   .   .   .

MARGINAL ANSWER

The First Amendment's provision denying power to Congress to pass laws respecting the establishment of religion is within the scope of the Fourteenth Amendment thus limiting the states and creating a wall of separation between church and state, according to Black in *Everson v. Board of Education.*

Here we must first determine whether such a law would be violative of the First Amendment as a law respecting an establishment of religion. On its face, it appears to be since it aids parents in sending their children to parochial schools.

However, there is much more to the issue than first appears. In *Everson v. Board of Education*, the court held that a statute that used taxpayer's money to aid children with transportation did not violate the due process clause of the 14th Amendment because the state law was passed to satisfy a public need. The court said that a state's power to legislate for a public need must not be curtailed. Similarly it can be argued here that Virginia must keep her parochial schools open, or else face the possibility that there will not be enough room in her public schools for all the children come September. The court also said in *Everson* that state power is no more to be used to handicap religions than it is to favor them; but, rather that the First Amendment requires a state to be a neutral in its relations with groups of religious believers and non-believers. However, *Everson* can be distinguished perhaps, because there the transportation services were so separate and marked off from the religious function while here the money for tuition determines whether or not the school will operate. As such, it is an integral part of the parochial school system—an indispensible part.

In *McCollum v. Board*, a released-time program was held unconstitutional because tax supported property was used for religious purposes and public officials had cooperated with religious authorities. In the instant case, however, the school board is not really cooperating with religious authorities since they are merely trying to ease the burden on the public schools by allowing the reimbursement to be paid to the parents, not to the church officials.

One of the other challenges in the *Everson* case was by a taxpayer who challenged the right of the board of education to reimburse parents for money expended by them for bus transportation on buses operated by the public transportation system. The Court rejected the taxpayer's contention stating that the use of the money there was a public use.

Later in *Board of Education v. Allen* members of a local board of education questioned the constitutionality of a state program *requiring* the local board to loan textbooks to students in parochial schools. The court held that this statute did not violate the religious clauses of the First Amendment because the

books went to *all* children—so, in other
words, it was a benefit to the children, and
not to the schools. In the instant case however, the money doesn't go to *all* parents, only to those who send their children to the parochial schools.

The Court has become increasingly liberal
as to the amount of injury that must be
shown where a plaintiff is raising issues involving the religious freedoms guaranteed by
the First Amendment. As an example, the
members of the local board of education were
held to have sufficient standing to challenge
on the rationale that if they refused to comply they would have faced expulsion from office and the state may have withheld funds
from their school districts.

The Federal Aid to Education Act of 1965
earmarked monies for use in textbooks etc.
to parochial schools. The challenge to this
was slow in coming. However in the *Flast*
case in 1968, the Court opened up a possible
challenge to the Act by modifying its stand-
ing-to-sue grounds. The new test for standing is that the taxpayer when challenging
must do so by saying that it involves some
other First Amendment freedoms.

So, therefore, the Court has loosened up on this question. Considering the changing court also, it is very difficult to say where the court is going on this question; however, I believe it somewhat of a safe bet that our taxpayer will prevail in this case remembering always that our constitutional law changes as our concept of justice changes.

.   .   .   .   .   .

COMMENT: This answer, although it states the general constitutional provisions involved and adequately explains the relevant case-law, does not carefully analyze the purposes and effects of the action of the Board of Education, and how they relate to religion. Nor does it present well-reasoned arguments as to just how and why the cases discussed should or should not apply to the Board's action here in view of its purposes and effects. The reasoning consists of a few suggested distinctions between other cases and this one and is quite general and vague in many respects. Most instructors would not grade this higher than "D".

CONSTITUTIONAL LAW (II)

(Open book exam—Two hours)

This question is in two parts. Answer each part separately.

A. Gopher Statutes 617.18 provides that "Every person who, with intent thereby to produce the miscarriage of a woman, unless the same is necessary to preserve her life, . . . shall

(1) prescribe, supply, or administer to a woman, whether pregnant or not, or advise or cause her to take, any medicine, drug, or substance; or

(2) use, or cause to be used, any instrument or other means—shall be guilty of abortion and punished by imprisonment in the state prison for not more than four years or in a county jail for not more than one year."

Gopher Statutes 617.19 provides that "A pregnant woman who takes any medicine, drug, or substance, or uses or submits to the use of any instrument or other means, with intent thereby to produce her own miscarriage, unless the same is necessary to preserve her life, . . . shall be punished by imprisonment in the state prison for not less than one year nor more than four years."

A physician, licensed to practice in the state of Gopher and specializing in obstetrics and gynecology, performed an abortion on a woman who contracted German Measles early in her pregnancy. The operation was performed during the fifth month of pregnancy in order to prevent the birth of a baby that was likely to be deformed.

The obstetrician was indicted, tried and convicted under Gopher Statutes 617.18 and sentenced to imprisonment for one year. No action has yet been taken by the County Attorney against the pregnant woman who voluntarily submitted to the abortion.

The conviction was affirmed by the Gopher Supreme Court. On appeal to the Supreme Court of the United States, how should that Court decide the case?

State, elaborate and *evaluate* the arguments for and against your answer, using the precedents and theories which you think have the most direct bearing on the question. You may and should apply a critical attitude concerning arguments, precedents and theories, but remember that sound criticism should encompass more than simple, unarticulated disagreement with particular cases or results.

If you think the facts given are inadequate in any way to enable you to answer the question, indicate what additional facts you would like to know and why you think these facts would have constitutional significance.

.   .   .   .   .   .

B.   You are a legislative assistant to U. S. Senator Brown of the state of Gopher. The Planned Parenthood League, the Population Control Association, and the Women's Rights Club in Gopher have urged the Senator to introduce two bills in Congress.

The first bill would legalize all abortions performed by licensed physicians in licensed hospitals throughout the United States within the first four months after conception and supersede all state laws to the contrary.

The second bill would establish federal birth control and abortion clinics in each state of the United States, to be founded by federal appropriations. At these clinics, physicians employed by the federal government would give birth control advice, dispense birth control pills and devices, and on request of the patient perform abortions during the first four months of pregnancy and voluntary sterilization operations on both men and women. The bill would relieve personnel employed by the clinics or individuals using the services of the clinics from any prohibition of any state law that might make the activities or uses of the clinics illegal.

The Senator asks you to study these proposals and to write a memorandum addressed to the following questions:

What are the various constitutional grounds of legislative power on which these proposals might reasonably be based? State and evaluate them. What kind of legislative findings would be useful in support of each proposal? How would the Supreme Court be likely to rule if the proposals were enacted and their constitutionality was challenged?

·   ·   ·   ·   ·   ·

COMMENT: The foregoing Constitutional Law Problem (II) really constitutes two distinct exam problems involving the same general policy question of legalizing abortion and birth control in different contexts of governmental action and power. (Problem A can also be regarded as one type of Criminal Law Problem.) Instructors frequently use this type of multiple-problem rather than completely separate problems to illustrate and

test the students' understanding of different legal aspects of a particular type of questionable behavior or action. Notice that separate answers are requested. When answering a problem like this be sure to deal adequately with each part. Do not concentrate so much on the first that you give superficial or incomplete answers to the other(s).

To permit easier comparison, the following sample answers are divided so that there is first a Good "A" Answer and Marginal Answer to Part A of the problem and then a similar pair of answers to Part B.

ANSWERS TO CONSTITUTIONAL LAW (II)

Part A

GOOD "A" ANSWER

A. The question in this first part is whether the state law prohibiting an abortion unless the mother's life is in danger deprives the person performing the operation of life, liberty, and property without due process of law, or of equal protection, under the fourteenth amendment. It is very similar to the question presented in *Griswold v. Conn.* concerning advising people about birth control, and is as difficult for me to deal with as it was for Douglas and the other five opinion writers.

If this was a deprivation of economic rights the court, under *Olson, Ferguson,* etc., would probably affirm the conviction and the constitutionality of the law without question. It is not.

Instead we are concerned with civil rights, the right of one to do what he wants with his or her body, the right to procreate and to stop procreation, to have and not have children. The first concern is whether these can be called liberties which can't be taken without due process. The second is whether if it is a liberty, it *was* taken with due process of law. The third is whether the classification of women whose lives are not endangered and those whose lives are in the balance constitutes an invidious discrimination which violates the equal protection clause of the fourteenth amendment.

With regard to the liberties to be protected, there are three approaches. First, the Black-Douglas "absolute incorporation" can be used. Under this approach, all of the amendments in the bill of rights, or at least 1–8, should be incorporated under the 14th

Amendment so that the state cannot deprive people of them just as the federal government cannot. This reasoning is that otherwise the court will have too much power to decide which rights cannot be restricted. Under this approach, one must look quite hard in 1–8 to find a right of which defendant is being deprived in this case. Perhaps under the first amendment you can say that the freedom of the doctor and the patient to associate was being denied. However, it was not; only the final operation was prohibited. The rights of privacy created under amendment 4, prohibiting illegal search and seizure, and the right against self-incrimination under amendment 5, may be used as Douglas used them. That is, he said that these guarantees of the right of privacy create, by emanations or "penumbras", a zone of privacy. This could then be taken to include privacy of the body, of the home, and non-interference with birth, which could lead to the unconstitutionality of the law. He also uses the ninth amendment which says that this isn't the total of private rights, but most jurists contend that this amendment can only limit the federal government.

Using the other approaches it is easier to find a violation. The Murphy-Rutledge con-

tention that the 14th amendment incorpo-
rates the bill of rights plus other fundamental rights is very helpful. A fundamental right definitely seems to include the
right to do what you want with your body.
Skinner says it includes the right to procreate, so there is little reason why it
shouldn't apply to the right not to have children. *Griswold* says it includes marital
rights and this seems to be a marital right,
and *Levy* and *Glona* say the relationship between child and parent is fundamental, and
this could possibly be regarded as such a
relationship.

The Frankfurter-Harlan approach, from
Adamson, Rochin and *Griswold,* is that "liberty" includes everything within the concept
of ordered liberty that all English-speaking
people must follow and prohibits any de-
preciations of liberty that are shocking to
the conscience". (Rochin). Preventing
children does not seem to be a concept that
all civilized countries would follow. The
Catholic religion which is espoused by a
large percentage of the people in these countries is opposed to it. Preventing a person
from having children already conceived is
also not shocking to the conscience. Yet,

the particular situation must be considered and also what the law really prevents. Invalidating the law does not prevent people from having children if they desire them and it can easily be contended that to have or not to have them is a personal choice which shouldn't be imposed on a person by law— that it is fundamental to have that choice. Moreover, the law not only prevents abortions of children expected to be normal but those who most likely will be infirm or deformed. In this case, it prevents birth of a baby who will probably be grotesque, unable to care for itself, and a great financial and mental burden to the family that could easily break up the total marital relationship and burden society with the child. To allow all of this may be shocking to the conscience. Allowing an abortion may fall within the concept of ordered liberty or the "fundamental freedoms." A law prohibiting such abortions may therefore be overbroad, even though a law prohibiting abortions of embryos expected to be normal would be constitutional.

Yet, even though there may be such a liberty to abort in certain cases some courts would say that a compelling state interest would still justify deprival of that liberty.

(*Skinner, McLaughlin, Loring* in the equal protection sphere and *Shapiro, Aptheker* with respect to due process). In this case such state interests may include preventing damage done to the mothers by unskilled practitioners, the increased promiscuity if unwed mothers can get abortions, and protecting the interests of the unborn child. All can be protected by a less broad statute. With respect to the first, only allowing abortions by licensed doctors or doctors skilled in the area would be enough of a restriction. With respect to the second, abortions of *unwed* mothers can be prohibited, and with respect to the third, abortions can be prohibited unless a doctor or a committee feels there is a good chance that the baby will be deformed. In that case, the baby has little interest in living. Yet, since this statute is overbroad, it should be deemed unconstitutional on its face if the rights previously considered, are regarded as fundamental (*Aptheker*). The fact that those rights are actually the rights of the patient rather than the doctor in this case is irrelevant because the patient, with such rights, needs a doctor to perform the operation safely.

The equal protection argument must also be considered, and if the rights previously stated are fundamental there must be a compelling state interest in discriminating against women whose lives aren't in danger even though their mental health may be by the birth of a deformed baby. The interest in allowing the abortion when the mother's life is in danger is that the legislature feels that the mother's life is more important than that of the child, even if the child could be born alive and healthy were not the abortion to result. They consider the fact that there wouldn't be a mother alive to take care of him and that the mother would be deprived of continued life, and her friends and family deprived of her companionship if no abortion were allowed while the child has no such friends and has never really lived so that people will suffer tragedy by his death. This may be compelling enough to justify the discrimination. However, it may not be, because a mother whose baby is deformed is likely to undergo mental illness and depression. She will likely suffer in her relations with others and her family ties will probably be disturbed. If she is considered more important than the child and the worth of the child must be lessened by his deformity, the reason for the discrimination may apply equally to the situation in this case, so that a law denying abortion in a situation like this violates the equal protection clause (*Skinner, Levy, Shapiro*) and is unconstitutional.

.   .   .   .   .   .

COMMENT: The excellence of this answer, its organization, writing style, clarity, depth of analysis, use of authorities, soundness and persuasiveness of reasoning should be sufficiently apparent. It would probably receive the top grade from most Constitutional Law teachers.

.   .   .   .   .   .

MARGINAL ANSWER

A. The statute is constitutionally applied to the physician because in performing the abortion, he had "intent to produce the miscarriage" of a woman; and he administered to a woman; and caused the use of "instruments" (his surgical tools). The matter of the woman's *consent* is not mentioned in the statute so it is irrelevant. The statute's one exception is if abortion is necessary to save the woman's life. This was not the purpose of the abortion here—it was to prevent the birth of a deformed baby. Thus, the elements necessary for conviction were present and the statute was constitutionally applied to him.

The statute is also constitutional on its face. It is not vague because the conduct punishable by this statute is stated specifically. *Wright v. Georgia.* The intent must be to produce a miscarriage of a woman, for other reasons than saving her life. The intent part of the statute is definite and gives a person of ordinary intelligence fair notice that his contemplated conduct is forbidden by law. *U. S. v. Harris.* The second requirement of the statute is some definite *act* on the part of the appellant, consummating his intent. This is met by either advising, supplying advice or by causing an instrument to be used. The second part is overt enough an act to satisfy the constitutional requirement. *U. S. v. O'Brien.* However, prescribing and advising someone to take medicine that causes an abortion might interfere with first amendment rights. Right to free speech is not an absolute right (*Schench v. U. S.; Gitlow v. N. Y.*) and the test, under *U. S. v. O'Brien,* is whether speech is combined with conduct—mere advice to cause the woman to take medicine may not be sufficient *overt* conduct (physical) to justify suspension of 1st Amendment freedom. Advocacy is never punishable unless there is the danger of imminent lawless action and it is likely to occur. *Brandenburg v. Ohio.* In such a statute as this, advice alone, especially from a confidential relationship (doctor-patient) can create an imminent danger of law violation and the likelihood that it will occur. Thus as applied to a doctor or special confidante, this statute is constitutional. But section (1), especially "advise or cause her to take" is open to multiple interpretation and not sufficiently definite to pass constitutional standards. *Wright v. George.* It may be *overdiscretionary,* as well as vague and too broad, and may be unconstitutional if this section of the statute is *subjectively* applied by the district attorney without further guidelines or standards. *Cox v. Louisiana.*

Thus, the statute is constitutional on its face and as applied—but the "advise" phrase might be stricken to prevent possible unconstitutional application in the future.

.   .   .   .   .   .

COMMENT: This answer is mainly concerned with Criminal Law issues of form and application of the statutes which are not

major problems of the constitutionality of the statutes. The answer mentions only briefly and obliquely First Amendment rights and does not really deal at all with the complex and controlling constitutional issues so ably brought out in the "A" answer. This answer is definitely not satisfactory and only marginally "D" rather than "F".

.   .   .   .   .   .

PART B (CONSTITUTIONAL LAW II)

GOOD "A" ANSWER

B. There are three major grounds on which the Federal Government could legislate on this problem, although it would normally be expected to be left to the state. With the liberalization in allowing federal regulation in areas formerly regarded as subject only to state regulation, each ground could be permissible.

First, the "clinic" law may be regarded as taxing and spending for the general welfare. The welfare clause has been interpreted by the court as giving Congress power to tax and spend for the general welfare, not limited to specified powers, provided such taxing and spending doesn't constitute a regulation. The states may argue, however, as they did in *Butler,* that the purpose of the spending is to curb a local problem and such problems are reserved to the states under the 10th Amendment. In *Butler,* the problem was farm production and relieving depressed farmers. Here it is birth control, a problem of health, morals and welfare. Yet the *Butler* test has been eroded by *Steward* which allowed relief of unemployment, usually regarded as a local problem and *Helvering* which allowed the social security tax to aid the aged. The reasoning of these latter cases seems valid since the problems are so widespread as to become national in scope.

Butler also said that the taxing and spending in that case was coercive on the farmers and therefore a regulation. In this case the people aren't being coerced or even enticed by the offer of money—as they were in Butler—to go to the clinics or to use the devices. Yet, it could be contended that the *states* are being regulated in that they are not being allowed to punish those disobeying their laws. Yet, in *Steward* the states were seemingly regulated to even a greater extent, since they were forced to establish unemployment compensation programs in order to keep their businessmen from being taxed for purposes which may not even be beneficial to the states. In this case the state is merely being prohibited from enforcing a law. This involves no expense whatsoever and no administration on the state's part.

In a period in which the Federal Government's taxing and spending powers are virtually unlimited (*U. S. v. Gerlach*) "except when the taxing or spending is being used for a general rather than a local purpose," it is doubtful that the Court would rule this legislation unconstitutional. In fact, even when the state spends for local improvements such as slum clearance, the court seems likely to validate such activity.

Even if the "clinic" law were regarded as regulatory and hence not valid under the taxing and spending clause, both it and the first law may be sustained on grounds that they are proper regulations "of commerce among the several states" within Congress's commerce clause powers. *Jones v. Laughlin, Darby, Feinblatt, Wichard, Heart of Atlanta,* and *Katzenbach v. McKlung* all said that if a local activity has such a close and substantial connection with commerce that it affects such commerce to a great extent, the local activity can be regulated and the state regulation in the same area preempted.

[*344*]

To sustain these clauses on these grounds, I would want to know the following facts. (1) Would such clinics and free abortions decrease the population to a significant extent. (2) If so would such decrease stimulate rather than depress the economy. If a lower population would result in less demand for goods, then the increased population without the law wouldn't harm commerce and may not be subject to regulation. If the decrease would mean the demand for goods wasn't so great that the prices weren't so high, so that inflation wasn't as likely to occur, the law may be valid. Moreover, if this decreased demand for employment would be such that everyone could be employed and the economy in this way remain stable, then commerce would be aided. If this law increased jobs at the clinic and perhaps for doctors so that these people would have more money to buy more goods and to travel more places, thereby generating more commerce, the law should again be validated. (These latter conditions would also be a reason for justifying taxing and spending since they improve the lot of most people, thereby constituting taxing and spending for the general welfare.) Finally, if some states allow abortions, clinics, etc., more people may be travelling to those states to enjoy the benefits and commerce in those states would be benefited at the expense of other commerce. The argument could then be made that this would constitute unfair competition which the commerce clause should prevent although it is a dubious contention, since the states that are losing out have the power to repeal their acts.

If these legislative findings were made, the court would probably sustain the regulations under the commerce clause, because the court in *Katzenbach v. McKlung* said that even if the reasons given by Congress (saying the activity regulated hurts commerce) are of questionable validity, the court's purpose isn't to question the wisdom of the findings. If they find there's a rational basis for them, this is sufficient.

Finally, under the 14th Amendment, when a state denies due process or equal protection to a person, the Congress can pass appropriate legislation to prevent such action. The major problem is to determine whether due process or equal protection have been denied. If the supreme court has already ruled that it has been there is no problem. Yet, if they haven't and the violation is questionable, one runs into the question presented in *Katzen-*

bach v. Morgan. In that case the court ruled that Congress itself can conclude that the activity in question violates the 14th Amendment and if there is a rational basis for such conclusion, the court cannot veto it. However, Harlan says Congress shouldn't have such power to function as a court and I tend to agree with him. In any case, I would want the legislature to find the infringements I have discussed in the answer to Part A of this problem, so the court could use them in deciding whether due process and equal protection had been denied.

.   .   .   .   .   .

COMMENT: This answer, like the one to Part A, is excellent. It pinpoints the constitutional bases for the desired Federal legislation and analyzes each systematically, thoroughly and persuasively on the basis of the relevant cases and the nature of the proposed congressional action.

.   .   .   .   .   .

MARGINAL ANSWER

B.   The constitutional grounds are based on fundamental law theory. Procreation is one of the fundamental rights of man. *Skinner v. Oklahoma.* There are some things a free government cannot do (*Cadder v. Bull*) and making it illegal to determine whether or not to procreate by abortion laws is in violation of the natural law of man. It is also a violation of privacy—and a reasonable analogy can be drawn from *Griswold v. Connecticut,* the case that said no state can deny an individual the right to prevent birth by contraceptive devices. How then, can government deny an individual the right to prevent birth by abortion before the foetus is a *viable* (separate entity) from its mother? This is an invasion of privacy and of due process of law. Thus, there are excellent constitutional grounds for the Senator's new proposal.

The second question is whether there is the requisite legislative power to accomplish the aims of the bill. The Congress has all the powers that are *"necessary and proper"* to achieve the ends of the Constitution. Since the constitutional basis is firm, the legislative power to enact is there. *McCulloch v. Maryland.* Legislative findings of a high number of deaths and serious injuries from illegal abortions and the public opinion as to whether they would consider abortion as an alternative birth control device if it was legalized would all be important findings contributing to the arguments for the new proposal. The Supreme Court might be moved to sustain the law on *public safety* basis (high number of serious injuries from illegal abortions) *Barnwell Bros., Maurer v. Hamilton*. Probably the supreme court would never reach the question because they would *not* sit as a super-legislator after the Congress had thoroughly investigated and passed the law. *Olson v. Nebraska ex rel. Ferguson*. The constitutionality of the law would and should be upheld because it is not a coercive or compulsory program (such as the abortion laws it would replace) but allows a flexible and reasonable approach to an individual problem.

.   .   .   .   .   .

COMMENT: The first paragraph of this answer is relevant to Part A of the problem and would have improved the answer to that part had it been included there. It is not relevant to Part B and demonstrates the writer's failure to grasp fully the distinction between constitutional limits on state powers and the extent of Federal powers under the U. S. constitution. The inadequacy of the remainder of the answer insofar as the issues in Part B are concerned is again obvious from a comparison with the "A" answer on Part B.

CRIMINAL LAW

GENERAL COMMENT: Because of the increased interest in and public concern over crime and law enforcement and the resultant changes and developments in many areas of "Criminal Law" in recent years, law school courses in this field are changing. It is therefore difficult to present "typical" exam problems in "Criminal Law" with any confidence that they will represent what first-year students will encounter in a law school course with that title.

Traditionally, law schools have offered a first-year course in "Criminal Law" which dealt primarily with the substantive elements and requirements, prescribed in the various bodies of state and Federal "criminal" statutes, for certain major types of "crimes", such as homicide, rape, assault, robbery, larceny, etc. and the penalties imposed for committing them (imprisonment, jail, fines, probation, etc.). For many years this law has been entirely statutory in this country, with case-law interpretations and constructions of the statutes. Each state has its own body of highly technical and detailed "criminal" statutes and case-law interpretations, differing in many respects from those of other states. The Federal Government, within its constitutional powers, also has its body of such substantive "criminal law".

Examination problems in such traditional courses thus ordinarily have referred to particular criminal statutes, described certain acts in specified circumstances, and asked for a determination or opinion as to whether such acts would come within and fulfill the specific requirements of one or more of these statutory "crimes". The illustrative problem and answers, given below, are of this type.

Some law schools, however, no longer give a basic first-year course in Criminal Law, but deal with various aspects of the subject in several later courses. Even those schools that have a first-year course generally devote much less time in it to the substantive statutory elements and requirements for specific crimes and more time to other areas of the subject such as criminal procedure, the constitutional problems of due process, search-and-seizure, privileges and immunities, crime prevention, rehabilitation, adequate legal representation of indigents charged with crime, etc. Sometimes, over two or three years, several courses in Criminal Law will be offered, each dealing with a different aspect of the subject. Sometimes the constitutional problems will be dealt with as a division of the course(s) in Constitutional Law and the Criminal Procedure problems will be studied as a division of Procedure.

In short, "Criminal Law" is now a broad area of law with numerous divisions taught in many schools at different times and in different courses. Thus, the following exam problem illustrates only one, traditional type and may not be representative of what to expect in many "Criminal Law" courses and examinations today. It was given on an exam in a one-quarter course in substantive criminal law at the University of Minnesota Law School where this traditional material was taught at the beginning of the second year.

PROBLEM

The Minnesota Statutes dealing with Homicide and Suicide in the Criminal Code of 1963, as amended, are as follows:

HOMICIDE AND SUICIDE

609.18 DEFINITION. For the purposes of sections 609.185 and 609.19, "premeditation" means to consider, plan or prepare for, or determine to commit, the act referred to prior to its commission.

[*1963 c 753 art 1 s 609.18*]

609.185 MURDER IN THE FIRST DE-GREE. Whoever does either of the following is guilty of murder in the first degree and shall be sentenced to imprisonment for life:

(1) Causes the death of a human being with premeditation and with intent to effect the death of such person or of another; or

(2) Causes the death of a human being while committing or attempting to commit rape or sodomy with force or violence, either upon or affecting such person or another.

[*1963 c 753 art 1 s 609.185*]

609.19 MURDER IN THE SECOND DE-GREE. Whoever causes the death of a human being with intent to effect the death of such person or another, but without premeditation, is guilty of murder in the second degree and may be sentenced to imprisonment for not more than 40 years.

[*1963 c 753 art 1 s 609.19*]

609.195 MURDER IN THE THIRD DE-GREE. Whoever, without intent to effect the death of any person, causes the death of another by either of the following means, is guilty of murder in the third degree and may be sentenced to imprisonment for not more than 25 years:

(1) Perpetrates an act eminently dangerous to others and evincing a depraved mind, regardless of human life; or

(2) Commits or attempts to commit a felony upon or affecting the person whose death was caused or another, except rape or sodomy with force or violence within the meaning of section 609.185.

[*1963 c 753 art 1 s 609.195*]

609.20 MANSLAUGHTER IN THE FIRST DEGREE. Whoever does any of the following is guilty of manslaughter in the first degree and may be sentenced to imprisonment for not more than 15 years or to payment of a fine of not more than $15,000, or both:

(1) Intentionally causes the death of another person in the heat of passion provoked by such words or acts of another as would provoke a person of ordinary self-control under like circumstances; or

(2) Causes the death of another in committing or attempting to commit a crime with such force and violence that death of or great bodily harm to any person was reasonably foreseeable, and murder in the first or second degree was not committed thereby; or

(3) Intentionally causes the death of another person because the actor is coerced by threats made by someone other than his co-conspirator and which cause him reasonably to believe that his act is the only means of preventing imminent death to himself or another.

[*1963 c 753 art 1 s 609.20*]

609.205 MANSLAUGHTER IN THE SECOND DEGREE. Whoever causes the death of another by any of the following means is guilty of manslaughter in the second degree and may be sentenced to imprisonment for not more than seven years or to payment of a fine of not more than $7,000, or both:

(1) By his culpable negligence whereby he creates an unreasonable risk, and consciously takes chances of causing death or great bodily harm to another; or

(2) By shooting another with a firearm or other dangerous weapon as a result of negligently believing him to be a deer or other animal; or

(3) By setting a spring gun, pit fall, deadfall, snare, or other like dangerous weapon or device; or

(4) By negligently or intentionally permitting any animal, known by him to have vicious propensities, to go at large, or negligently failing to keep it properly confined, and the victim was not at fault.

[*1963 c 753 art 1 s 609.205*]

609.21 CRIMINAL NEGLIGENCE RESULTING IN DEATH. Whoever operates a vehicle as defined in Minnesota Statutes, Section 169.01, Subdivision 2, or an aircraft or watercraft, in a grossly negligent manner and thereby causes the death of a human being not constituting murder or manslaughter is guilty of criminal negligence in the operation of a vehicle resulting in death and may be sentenced to imprisonment for not more than five years or to payment of a fine of not more than $5,000, or both.

[*1963 c 753 art 1 s 609.21*]

The following fact situation is a slightly altered version of the facts as stated in People v. Caruso, 246 N.Y. 437, 159 N.E. 390. Assuming these facts in Minnesota, for what if anything would you, as a prosecutor, prosecute Mr. Caruso, what verdict or verdicts would you anticipate being submitted to the jury and what result would you expect the jury to reach? Explain.

Francesco Caruso, an illiterate Italian, thirty-five years old, came to this country about 1951. He worked as a laborer, and in the early part of 1967 was living with his wife and six small children in an apartment in Minneapolis. On Friday, February 11th, one of these children, a boy of six, was ill with a sore throat. That day and the next he treated the boy with remedies bought at a drug store. The child grew worse and at ten o'clock of the night of the 12th he sent for a Doctor Pendola, who had been recommended to him, but with whom he was not acquainted.

What followed depends upon a statement made by Caruso.

Sometime between ten-thirty and eleven in the evening Dr. Pendola arrived. The child had diphtheria. Caruso was sent out

to buy some anti-toxin, and when he returned the doctor administered it. He then gave
Caruso another prescription with instructions as to its use and left, promising to return in the morning.

Caruso watched the child all night, giving
remedies every half hour. "About four
o'clock in the morning," he testified, "my
child was standing up to the bed, and asked
me to, he says, 'Papa' he said 'I am dying.'
I say that time, I said, 'You don't die.' I
said 'I will help you every time.' The same
time that child he will be crazy—look like
crazy, that time—don't want to stay any
more inside. All I can do, I keep my child
in my arms, and I held him in my arms from
four o'clock until eight o'clock in the morning. After eight o'clock in the morning the
poor child getting worse—the poor child in
the morning he was"—(slight interruption
in the testimony while the defendant apparently stops to overcome his emotion).
"The poor child that time, and he was asking me, 'Papa,' he said, 'I want to go and
sleep.'

"So I said, 'All right, Giovie, I will put you
in the sleep.' I take my Giovie and I put him
in the bed, and he started to sleep, to wait

until the doctor came, and the doctor he never came. I waited from ten o'clock, the doctor he never came." Then after trying in vain to get in touch with the doctor he sent for an ambulance from a drug store. "When I go home I seen my child is got up to the bed that time, and he says to me, 'Papa, I want to come with you.' I take my child again up in my arms and I make him look to the back yard to the window. He looked around the yard about a couple of minutes and after, when he looked around, he says to me, 'Papa, I want to go to sleep again.'

"I said 'All right, Giovie, I will put you in the sleep.' I put my child on the bed. About a few seconds my child is on the bed, my child says to me, he says, 'Papa, I want to go to the toilet.'

"I said, 'All right, Giovie, I will take you to the toilet. So I was trying to pick up the child and make him go to the toilet, when I held that child I felt that leg—that child started to shake up in my arms. My wife know about better than me—I cannot see good myself in the face, so she tell what kind of shakes he do, and she has told me, she says, "Listen, Frank, why, the child has died already." '

"I said, 'All right, you don't cry. No harm, because you make the child scared.' That time I go right away and put the child on the bed. When I put the child, before I put my hand to the pillow, my child said to me, 'Good-bye, Papa, I am going already.'

"So that time I put my hands to my head— I said, 'That child is dead. I don't know what I am going to do myself now.' That time I never said nothing, because I said, 'Jesus, my child is dead now. Nobody will get their hands on my child.' "

About twelve o'clock Dr. Pendola arrived. The child had been dead for some time. He was told and then Caruso says the doctor laughed and he "lost his head." The probability is there was, from one cause or another, some twitching of the facial muscles that might be mistaken for a smile.

Then followed some talk. Caruso accused the doctor of killing his child. The doctor denied it. Caruso attacked him in anger, choked him until he fell to the floor, then went to a closet ten or twelve feet away, took a knife and stabbed him twice in the throat, so killing him. Caruso then took his family to the janitor's apartment downstairs, and himself went to his brother's house in St. Paul where he was arrested that night. He made no attempt whatever to conceal the facts of the homicide.

Caruso says that when he was buying the anti-toxin the druggist told him that the dose was too large for a child of the age of his son. This he told the doctor. The latter was indignant and paid no heed to the warning. The druggist denied any such conversation and apparently the dose was proper. Immediately after the death Caruso told an ambulance surgeon that Dr. Pendola had killed his child by an injection; and also complained of his delay in not coming that morning.

.   .   .   .   .   .

ANSWERS TO CRIMINAL LAW

GOOD "A" ANSWER

There will obviously be problems with this case because of the sympathetic image the defendant may convey to a jury.

§ 609.185 (Murder In The First Degree) does not seem applicable on the stated facts. For there to be murder in the first degree there must be premeditation and the necessary intent to kill. Many courts have said that premeditation may be found where the formation of the intent to kill is followed immediately by the homicidal act. In most states no particular length of time is necessary; a mere instant of reflection is sufficient. But other states such as Minnesota and California require more. The obvious attempt by the drafters of the statute is to make premeditation something more than mere intent to kill. There must be a weighing of alternative courses of action so it (the homicidal act) results from real and substantial reflection. Thus, it is my belief that first degree murder would not be an appropriate charge in this case and if made, it might be prejudicial.

Defendant's actions seem to come within the scope of § 609.19 Murder In The Second Degree, which is murder with intent to cause death but without premeditation. It would seem that the requisite intent is present. Caruso strangled the doctor until helpless, then went and got a knife and stabbed him to death.

Under § 609.02(9) [4] the words "with intent" mean that the actor either has a purpose to do the thing or cause the result specified or believes that his act, if successful, will cause that result. This is, however, a jury question and under present law it could be based upon permissible inference. Here a jury could find intent to effectuate the death of the doctor.

§ 609.195(1) Murder In The Third Degree, is also a possibility. That is, without intent to kill the doctor he perpetrates "an act eminently dangerous to others and evincing a depraved mind, regardless of human life." But there are very real problems here, as this section has been held by Minnesota courts to apply only to acts dangerous to several others and not directed at any one particular person. The Minnesota court has said "it is necessary that the act was committed without special design upon the particular person or persons with whose murder he is charged." Thus it would seem that third degree murder would be inapplicable to the situation at hand.

As an alternative, Manslaughter In The First Degree could be properly charged (§ 609.20(1)). The requirements are that he *intentionally* causes the death of another in heat of passion provoked by such words or acts as would provoke a person of ordinary self-control under like circumstances. Again there is an intent problem. As stated above, it would seem there was sufficient evidence to prove intent.

The problem, in finding manslaughter, lies in whether the doctor's acts are such as would provoke an ordinary man under like circumstances. Probably not. It seems incredulous that the doctor would smile at the boy's death. As explained, it was probably some facial twitch. Also the druggist denied telling Caruso that the prescription was wrong. However, Caruso, having a language problem, may have misunderstood. It would seem definitely that the defendant acted in the heat of passion, but was the passion reasonable? This is an objective standard and it seems that the average man would not so react. But, under the facts of the case, this is a jury question. I feel a jury might (if defendant is a sympathetic enough person) find manslaughter.

Because of the foregoing, I would submit Second-Degree Murder, First Degree Manslaughter and, of course, Not Guilty to the jury. I expect a verdict of Murder In The Second Degree because the jury is likely to find an intentional killing and also that the defendant was not reasonably provoked.

MARGINAL ANSWER

In determining for what to prosecute, several factors are relevant. First, the evidence as given by the defendant may or may not be believed by the jury. It appears that the jury could believe that he exaggerates and gets his facts confused. For example, what did the druggist really say and what did the doctor really do. Hence the credibility of his testimony is open to attack. Further, defendant's eyes were bad and perhaps incapable of detecting the expression on the doctor's face. With the possibility of highly conflicting testimony in mind, I shall proceed.

I would prosecute defendant for first degree murder, realizing, however, the possibility of sufficient provocation which would mitigate to first degree manslaughter.

The first problem is the requisite premeditation under § 609.185. It appears that there is a good chance of convincing the jury, through testimony, that when defendant realized that the child was dying and then died, he immediately blamed the doctor and began premeditating the killing. The intent to cause death § 609.02(9) (4), appears from his objective acts (not concealing homicide for example) and does not appear controverted by his testimony. As long as it is likely that the jury will convict for first degree murder, the instruction should be given.

With the verdict of guilty of first degree murder, pursuant to § 609.04 other verdicts should be submitted. These include:

(1) Second degree murder. It is possible that the jury will not find premeditation but upon the evidence a judge should find the required intent.

(2) A first-degree manslaughter, § 609.20 (1), instruction must be given. Provocation is a strong defense for the defendant if he can show that the doctor's omission—failure in duty to tend to a dying patient, prescribing incorrect dosage and breach of duty owed as a physician—was the cause of his son's death and therefore the precipitating factor in causing him to act in the heat of passion. The murder death of a child is the type of provocation intended to come within § 609.20 (1). Note, however, that it is not a justification under § 609.065. The prosecution will try to prove no justification by proving the father's omission—breach of duty to child to obtain another physician or to call deceased by showing that the necessary causation be-

tween the doctor's absence or prescriptions caused the death of the child. Under the latter circumstances, the heat of passion would seem unreasonable. Even if the jury finds sufficient provocation, the prosecution will try to prove that sufficient time had elapsed, so that there was a sufficient "cooling off" period.

(3) Aggravated assault, § 609.225, is also a possibility.

The verdict I would expect is guilty of § 609.20(1). The jury would be likely to find sufficient evidence of provocation. Society and legislation seem to protect the parent-child relationship and recognize the closeness of it. Certainly a code which allows provocation as a mitigating force when rape has been committed upon a close relative would allow provocation upon a reasonable belief by a parent that another killed his child. Even in light of attacks upon causation and credibility it seems difficult, from the point of view of practical experience, to say that the jury will not exercise its discretion to find the objective reasonableness standard met. That is, an ordinary man of ordinary mind would have been liable to act in the same way as defendant.

. . . . . .

COMMENT: The first answer more clearly identifies the three alternative statutes; more clearly states what issue there is with regard to the applicability of each of the three alternative statutes; expresses a judgment as to how the particular issue is likely to be resolved; and comes to an overall judgment about the case reflecting, in the process, an awareness of the relative functions of the judge and the jury.

The second answer is much less precise, vacillates a great deal, and does not give any clear indication of the writer's judgment as to how the basic questions ought to be resolved.

INDEX

References are to Pages

ABSENCES
Class attendance, 70

ACCURACY
Objectives, law examinations, 102

ACTIONS
Briefing cases, 53

ADMINISTRATIVE BOARDS AND COMMISSIONS
Rules and procedures, law study, law schools, 6

ADMINISTRATIVE LAW
Rules and procedures, etc., 12

ADMINISTRATORS
Lawyers, 18

ADVICE
Law practice, 18

ADVOCATES
Attorneys, 19

AGENTS AND AGENCIES
Governmental agencies, employment, legal counsel, 18
Law examination, agency, contracts cases, 172, 173
Law practice, 18

ANALYSIS
Court's arguments and conclusions, 49
Law examinations, problem analysis, 121 et seq.

INDEX

ANALYSIS—Cont'd
Legal documents and law-books, 23
Legal problems, object, law study, 20
Memorandum, proposed legislation, 286 et seq.
Object, law study, 20

ANSWERS
Generally, 101 et seq.
Agency, contract cases, 174 et seq.
Check-lists, grading answers, 134 et seq.
Civil procedure, law examination, 305 et seq.
Closed-book property law school examinations, 271 et seq.
Constitutional law question, examination, 318 et seq.
Contracts problem, law examination, 150 et seq.
Remedies problem, law examinations, 138 et seq.
Criminal law, law school examinations, 362 et seq.
Illustrative problem questions with sample answers, law examinations, 129 et seq.
Law examinations, writing, 118 et seq.
Planning law examination answers, 126, 127
Real property law examinations, 258 et seq.
Grading, 252 et seq.
Remedies, answer, contracts remedies problem, 138 et seq.
Sample answers, illustrative problem questions with sample answers, 129 et seq.
Tort questions, law examinations, 192 et seq., 212 et seq., 231 et seq.
What law examiner looks for, 108 et seq.

APPELLATE COURTS
Normal functions, 42

AREAS
Law, areas of law, 11

ARGUMENTS
Challenges by good lawyers, 26
Reading cases, 44

INDEX
References are to Pages

ARGUMENTS—Cont'd
Reading court's argument, 48
Review with other students, 87, 88
Written and oral argument, 27

ASSAULT AND BATTERY
Torts, examination problem, general comment, 184

ASSUMPTIONS
Challenges by good lawyer, 26

ATTENDANCE
Class attendance, 62 et seq.
    Absences, 70
    Importance, 66 et seq.

ATTORNEYS
    Generally, 17 et seq.
Administrators, 18
Advocates, 19
Analysis, legal documents and law-books, 23
Draft, proposed legislation, comment, 290, 291
Experts, 18
Government officials, 18
Importance of language, 22, 23
Legislators, 18

BAR ASSOCIATIONS
Law reform and law improvement activities, 19

BAR EXAMINATIONS
Tests, problems-questions, 105

BELIEFS
Ingredients of law, 22

BOOKS
    Generally, 30 et seq.
Casebooks, 31 et seq.
Cases in casebooks, 3A
Contents, subject matter of law, 23

BOOKS—Cont'd
Law books, 30 et seq.
Subject matter of law, 23

BRIEFS
Generally, 51 et seq.
Canned briefs, 60, 61
Sample brief, 58, 59

CASEBOOKS
See Books, generally, this index

CASES
Generally, 31 et seq.
Briefing cases, 51 et seq.
Reading cases, 40 et seq.

CHECK-LISTS
Grading answers, law examinations, 134 et seq.

CIVIC ORGANIZATIONS
Law reform and law improvement activities, 19

CIVIL ACTIONS
Self-defense, 57

CIVIL LAW
Areas of law, 11
Distinctions between areas of law, 13
Rules applicable to, 13

CIVIL PROCEDURE
Law examination question, 304, 305
Answer, 310 et seq.

CLASSIFICATIONS
Substantive, remedial and procedural law, 82

CLASSWORK
Generally, 62 et seq.

CLIENTS
Object of law study, advising, 20

INDEX

References are to Pages

COMMENTS

Law exam problems, 101 et seq.
  Civil procedure, answer, 308
  Illustrative problem questions with sample answers, 129 et seq.

COMMUNICATIONS

Objectives, law examinations, 102

COMPENSATION AND SALARIES

Law practice, 18

CONCEPTS

Ingredients of law, 22

CONCLUSIONS

Answers, law exam questions, 115
Challenges by good lawyers, 26
Ingredients of law, 22
Object, law study, 20
Reading court's conclusions, 48

CONSTITUTIONAL LAW

Law examination question, 316 et seq.
Rules and procedures, etc., 12

CONTRACTS

Law examination problem, 148 et seq.
  Answer to contracts problem, 150 et seq.
    Contracts remedies problem, 138 et seq.
Remedies, answer, contracts remedies problem, law examination, 138 et seq.
Rules and procedures, etc., 12

CONTROVERSIES

Reading cases, 47
  Brief statement, 41
Study and class discussion, 20, 21

COUNSEL

See Attorneys, generally, this index

INDEX

COUNSELING
Law practice, 18

COURTS
Judges presiding over, 18

CRIMINAL LAW
Areas of law, 11
Distinctions between areas of law, 13
Law school courses, 350 et seq.
Law school examinations, 350 et seq.
  Procedure, examination problems, 350 et seq.
Rules and procedures, etc., 12
Self-defense, 57
Statutes, general comment, 350 et seq.
Statutory or administrative prohibitions, 12

DECEIT
Examination problem, general comment, 184

DECISIONS
Answers, law exam questions, 115
Briefing cases, 53
Court's decision, 46
Object of law study, how to find, 20
Statement of court's decision, 46
Subject matter of law, 23
Trial court decisions, 36

DEDUCTIVE REASONING
Generally, 44, 45

DEEDS AND CONVEYANCES
Law examination questions and problems, 252 et seq.

DEFAMATION
Examination problem, general comment, 184

DEFINITIONS
Law, 5

INDEX
References are to Pages

DIAGRAM
Interrelationship between laws, 15

DIGESTS
Subject matter of law, 23

DISCUSSIONS
Review with other students, 87, 88

DISPUTES
Study and class discussion, 20, 21

DOCUMENTS
Law practice, preparation, 18
Preservation of law, 23
Reading skills, 24 et seq.
Writing skills, 27

DRAFTS
Attorneys, proposed legislation, comment, 290, 291
Instruments, object of law study, 20

ECONOMIC INTERESTS
Protection by lawyers, 19

ENCYCLOPEDIAS
Subject matter of the law, 23

ESTATES AND TRUSTS
Rules and procedures, etc., 12

EVALUATION
Memorandum, proposed legislation, 286 et seq.
Objectives, law examinations, 102

EXAMINATIONS
Generally, 101 et seq.
See, also,
Problems, generally, this index
Questions, generally, this index
Agency, contracts cases, 172, 173
Answers, generally, this index

INDEX

References are to Pages

EXAMINATIONS—Cont'd

Assault and battery, general comment, 184

Check-lists, grading answers, 134 et seq.

Civil procedure questions, 304, 305

Comments,
> Criminal law, general comment, 350 et seq.
> Illustrative problem questions with sample comments, 129 et seq.

Constitutional law questions, 316 et seq.

Contracts problem, 148 et seq.
> Answer to contracts problem, 150 et seq.
> Remedies problems, 138 et seq.

Criminal law, 350 et seq.

Deceit, general comment, 184

Defamation, general comment, 184

False imprisonment, general comment, 184

Illustrative problem questions with sample answers and comments, 129 et seq.

Negligence, general comment, 184

Objectives, 102

Personal property, problems and questions, 252 et seq.

Planning examination answers, 126, 127

Preparation, study for law examinations, 95 et seq.

Procedure, 304, 305

Professor's check-list, grading answers, 134 et seq.

Property, 251 et seq.
> Closed-book examination, 266 et seq.

Real property, problems and questions, 252 et seq.

Remedies problem, answer, contracts remedies problem, 138 et seq.

Sample answers and comments with illustrative problem questions, 129 et seq.

Study for examinations, 95 et seq.

Torts, 184 et seq.
> Answers to tort problems, 192 et seq., 212 et seq., 231 et seq.
>> Question, 207 et seq., 228 et seq.

INDEX

References are to Pages

EXAMINATIONS—Cont'd
What examiner looks for in answers to problem questions, 108 et seq.
Writing answers, 118 et seq.

EXPERTS
Attorneys, 18

EXPLANATIONS
Purpose of book, 1

FACTS
Briefing cases, 53

FALSE IMPRISONMENT
Examination problems, general comment, 184

FEDERAL
Rules and procedures, law study, law schools, 6

FREEDOM
Individual freedom, objective of law, 8
Protections by lawyers, 19

GOVERNMENT OFFICIALS
Lawyers, 18

GRADING
Answers, real property law examinations, 252 et seq.
Check-list, grading answers to law examination, 134 et seq.
Statutory language, test of student's ability, 291

HEARING
Representation of client, object of law study, 20

HOMICIDE
Law school examinations, 352 et seq.

HORNBOOKS
Using student hornbooks, 73 et seq.

INDEX
References are to Pages

HYPOTHETICAL QUESTIONS
Generally, 64

IDEAS
Ingredients of the law, 22

ILLUSTRATION
Problem questions with sample answers and comments, law examinations, 129 et seq.

IMPORTANCE
Class attendance, 66 et seq.

INDUCTIVE REASONING
Generally, 44, 45

INFORMATION
Purpose of book, 1

INSTRUCTION
Case method of legal instruction, 32

INSTRUCTORS
Analysis, standards for grading real property law examination, 253 et seq.
Check-list in grading answers to law examination, 134 et seq.

INSTRUMENTS
Drafting, object of law study, 20
Reading skills, 24 et seq.
Writing skills, 27

INTENT
Purpose of book, 1

INTRODUCTION
Generally, 1 et seq.
Law exam problems, answers and comments, 101 et seq.

INDEX

ISSUES
Answers, law exam questions, 115
Briefing cases, 53
Check-lists, professor grading answers to law examination, 134 et seq.
Reading cases, 44, 46
Torts, law examination problems, 184

JUDGES
Presiding over courts, 18

JUDGMENTS
See Decisions, generally, this index

KNOWLEDGE
Objectives of law examinations, 102

LABORATORY
Law library, lawyer's and law student's laboratory, 23, 30

LANGUAGE
Importance to lawyers and law students, 22, 23
Test of skills, 108
    Student's ability to read statutory language, 291

LAW
Areas of law, 11
Defined, 5
Object of law study, 20, 21

LAW BOOKS
See Books, generally, this index

LAW EXAMINATIONS
See Examinations, generally, this index

LAW LIBRARY
Laboratory of lawyer and law student, 30
Warehouse, workshop and laboratory, 23

INDEX

LAW PRACTICE
Generally, 18

LAW REVIEWS
Subject matter of law, 23

LAW SCHOOLS
Generally, 17 et seq.
Courses, criminal law, general comment, 350 et seq.
Criminal law courses, general comment, 350 et seq.
Law study in law schools, 5 et seq.
Object of law study, 20, 21

LAW STUDENTS
See Students, generally, this index

LAW STUDY
See Study, generally, this index

LAWYERS
See Attorneys, generally, this index

LEGAL PROCESS
Law study involves, 8

LEGAL PROFESSION
See Attorneys, generally, this index

LEGISLATION
Memorandum, analysis and evaluation of proposed
    legislation, 286 et seq.

LEGISLATORS
Lawyers, 18

LITERATURE
Constitution of legal literature, 23

LIVES
Protection by lawyers, 19

MANSLAUGHTER
Law school examinations, 354, 355 et seq.

INDEX
References are to Pages

MEMORANDUM
Analysis and evaluation, proposed legislation, 286 et seq.
Torts, law examination, 186 et seq.

METHODS
Teaching methods, 62 et seq.

MURDER
Law school examinations, 352 et seq.

NATIONAL REPORTER SYSTEM
Reports published in, 37, 38

NECESSITY
Publication of book, 2

NEGLIGENCE
Examination problem, general comment, 184

NEGOTIATIONS
Object of law study, 20

NOTES
Taking notes, classwork, 62, 63

OBJECTIVES
Law, objectives of law, 8
Law study, object of law study, 20, 21
Methods and objectives of law study and examinations, 3

OFFICIAL REPORTS
Generally, 37

OPEN-BOOK
Constitutional law examination, 328 et seq.

OPINIONS
See, also, Decisions, generally, this index
Casebooks, 34
Object of law study, writing, 20
Written and oral opinions by attorneys, 27

INDEX
References are to Pages

ORDER
Briefing cases, 53

OUTLINES
Generally, 89 et seq.

OWNERSHIP
Property, law examinations questions, 252 et seq.

PARTIES
Torts, law examination problems, 184

PERSONAL PROPERTY
Law examination questions and problems, 252 et seq.

PREDICTIONS
Probable solutions of legal problems, 21

PREMISES
Challenges by good lawyer, 26

PRIVATE LAW
Areas of law, 11
Classifications, 82
Distinctions between areas of law, 13
Rules applicable, 13
Torts,
    Law examination questions, 184 et seq.
    Major division, 184

PRIVILEGES AND IMMUNITIES
Property rights, law examination questions, 252 et seq.

PROBLEMS
Answers, generally, this index
Attorneys, expert legal problem solvers, 19
Bar examinations, 2, 105
Contracts, law examination problem, 148 et seq.
    Remedies, 131 et seq.
Drafts of bills, comment, 290, 291
Hypothetical problems, 64

INDEX
References are to Pages

PROBLEMS—Cont'd
Illustrative problem questions with sample answers
    and comments, law examinations, 129 et seq.
Law examinations, 101 et seq.
    Analysis of problem, 121 et seq.
    Answers, 101 et seq.
        Contracts remedies problem, 138 et seq.
    Contracts remedies problem, answer, 138 et seq.
    Examine problems and bar examination problems,
        2
    Reading, 120
    Reading problem, 120
    Remedies, answers to contracts remedies prob-
        lem, 138 et seq.
    What law examiner looks for in answers to prob-
        lems, 108 et seq.
Lawyers, solvers, 19
Object of law study, 20
Property, law examinations, 252 et seq.

PROCEDURAL LAW
Classifications, 82
Interrelationship between laws, 14
Types of legal rules, 8

PROCEDURES
See Rules and Procedures, generally, this index

PROFESSION
See Attorneys, generally, this index

PROPERTY
Law examinations, 251 et seq.
    Closed-book, 266 et seq.

PROTECTION
Individual protection, objective of law, 8

PUBLIC LAW
Areas of law, 11

[*383*]

INDEX
References are to Pages

PUBLIC LAW—Cont'd
Classifications, 82
Distinction between areas of law, 13
Rules and procedures, etc., 12
Statutory or administrative prohibitions, 12

PUBLICATIONS
Preservation of legal publications, 23
Reading skills, 24 et seq.

PUPILS
See Students, generally, this index

QUESTIONS
Generally, 102 et seq.
Answers, generally, this index
Bar examinations, 105
Contracts remedies, 131 et seq.
Hypothetical questions, 64
Illustrative problem questions with sample comments
and answers, 129 et seq.
Law examinations, 102 et seq.
Torts, 207 et seq.
Property, 252 et seq.
Torts, 184 et seq., 207 et seq., 228 et seq.
What law examiner looks for in answer, 108 et seq.

READING
Cases, 40 et seq.
Court's argument, 48
Problem, law examinations, 120
Skills, 24 et seq.
Supplementary reading, 70 et seq.

REAL PROPERTY
Answers to law examination, 258 et seq.
Law examinations, problems and questions, 252 et seq.

REASONS AND REASONING
Briefing cases, 53

INDEX

References are to Pages

REASONS AND REASONING—Cont'd
Case method, legal instruction, 32
Object of law study, 20
Reading court's reasoning, 48

RECORDS
Subject matter of law, 23

REMEDIAL LAW
Classifications, 82
Interrelationship between laws, 14
Types of legal rules, 9

REMEDIES
Contracts remedies, problem, 131 et seq.
    Answer, law examinations, 138 et seq.
Rules and procedures, etc., 12

REPORTS
Cases reproduced in casebooks, 35
National reporter system, 37, 38
Preservation of law, 23
Selected reports, 38
Subject matter of law, 23

REPRESENTATION
Client in law suit object of law study, 20

RESEARCH
Object of law study, 20

REVIEW
    Generally, 78 et seq.
Day-to-day review, 79 et seq.
Discussions and arguments, 87, 88
Periodic review, 82 et seq.
Students, review with other students, 87, 88

RULES AND PROCEDURES
Areas of law, 12
Briefing cases, 52

[*385*]

INDEX

References are to Pages

RULES AND PROCEDURES—Cont'd
Civil law, 13
Ingredients of law, 22
Law, study in law schools, 6
Object of law study, how to find, 20
Private law, 13
Self-defense, 57
Study of law in law schools, 6
Types of legal rules, 8

SAFETY
Protection by lawyers, 19

SAMPLES
Briefs, sample briefs, 58, 59
Illustrative problem questions with sample answers and comments, law examinations, 129 et seq.

SCHOOLS
See Law Schools, generally, this index

SELECTED REPORTS
Generally, 38

SERVICES
Law practice, 18

SKILLS
Generally, 22 et seq.
Objectives of law examinations, 103, 104
Reading skills, 24 et seq.
Writing skills, 27 et seq.

SOCIAL ORDER
Objectives of law, 8

SOLUTIONS
Object of law study, 20

STANDARDS
Attorneys, professional standards, 19
Professional law schools, 17

INDEX

References are to Pages

STARE DECISIS
Principle, 33

STATE
Rules and procedures, law study in law schools, 6

STATE REPORTS
Generally, 37

STATEMENTS
Questions for court, reading cases, 44
Reading cases, statement of facts, 43

STATUTES
Closed-book property law examination with selected
statutes, 266 et seq.
Criminal law, general comment, 350 et seq.
Subject matter of law, 23

STRICT LIABILITY
Torts, law examination problems, general comment,
184

STUDENTS
Analysis, legal documents and law-books, 23
Hornbooks, using textbooks and hornbooks, 73 et seq.
Importance, language to law students, 22, 23
Language, importance, 22, 23

STUDY
Case method of law study, 31
Law examinations, 95 et seq.
Law study in law school, 5 et seq.
Legal documents and law-books, 23
Method, case method, 31
Object of law study, 20, 21
What law study is all about, 5 et seq.

SUBDIVISION
Areas of law, 11

INDEX

References are to Pages

SUBJECT MATTER
Law, 23

SUBSTANTIVE LAW
Classifications, 82
Interrelationship between laws, 14
Types of legal rules, 8

SUGGESTIONS
Purpose of book, 1

SUMMARY
Professor's summary, check-list, grading answers to
  law examinations, 134 et seq.

SUPPLEMENTARY READING
Generally, 70 et seq.

TAXATION
Rules and procedures, etc., 12

TESTS
Bar examinations, 105
Student's ability to read statutory language, comment,
  291

TEXTBOOKS
Subject matter of law, 23
Using student textbooks, 73 et seq.

TITLE
Property, law examination questions, 252 et seq.

TOOLS
Generally, 22 et seq.

TORTS
Law examination question, 184 et seq., 207 et seq., 228
  et seq.
    Answer to torts question, 192 et seq., 212 et seq.,
      231 et seq.
Rules and procedures, etc., 12

INDEX
References are to Pages

TRANSFERS
Real property, law examination questions, 252 et seq.

TREATISES
Subject matter of law, 23

TYPES
Questions on law exams, 102 et seq.

UTILITIES
Rules and procedures, etc., 12

WAREHOUSE
Law library, lawyer's and law student's warehouse, 23

WILLS
Rules and procedures, etc., 12

WORKSHOP
Law library, lawyer's and law student's workshop, 23

WRITING
Answers, law examinations, 118 et seq.
Object of law study, opinion writing, 20
Skills, writing skills, 27 et seq.
Test, writing skills, 108